5.00

tortured linguistic logic p.7

re Amharic, p.31

SHEBA
SLEPT
HERE

Trevor Hudson

Sheba Slept Here

by Alan Caillou

ABELARD-SCHUMAN
AN Intext PUBLISHER

New York • *London*

NEW YORK
Abelard-Schuman
Limited
257 Park Avenue So.
10010

LONDON
Abelard-Schuman
Limited
158 Buckingham Palace Road SW1
and
24 Market Square Aylesbury

Published on the same day in Canada by Longman Canada Limited.

Printed in the United States of America

Library of Congress Cataloging in Publication Data

————
Sheba slept here.

1. Ethiopia—Description and travel—1945–
I. Title.
DT378.L9   1973   916.3'04'6   72–9544
ISBN 0–200–04000–6

SHEBA
SLEPT
HERE

1

Even the beginnings had overtones of comedy.

That an out-of-work actor in London should suddenly find himself Chief of Police in Ethiopia is remarkable enough; but the whole thing came about through deviousness (and perhaps a little stupidity) on my part, and stupidity (and perhaps a little deviousness) on the part of the War Office.

The war in Europe was over. It was the spring of 1945.

In the Far East, the Americans had politely, but firmly, told the Government in Whitehall that they, and they alone, would take care of Japan. Spheres of interest, balance of power, all the old clichés (which perhaps had caused World Wars I and II) were brought into use. . . . And finally, reluctantly, they accepted a token force of the Royal Navy, and that was that.

But I was Army, and the army was at a loose end. Men were

being demobilized, and the effect of this sudden deluge on the labor market was appalling.

The British economy had been shattered by six years of war that had cost us over twelve billion pounds sterling (while in the same period the national revenue was a little under five and a half billion); many of the great cities lay in ruins; the people were tired and worn out; and in short, the halcyon days were over.

In the army, we were permitted to sign on for two more years, or to resign our commissions at once and take our chances.

I chose to do both; that's where the deviousness came in. I "lost" the contracts they sent me for signature, three, four, five times, and managed to keep myself in a state of suspended animation, still on the payroll but able to opt out at a moment's notice if something worth while turned up. But half of London's theaters were closed, or destroyed, and there wasn't much call for actors. I made the rounds.

And then, while I was being signed up for a short-run play in the outskirts of the City, my wife called up and said: "The War Office is looking for you, you'd better get in touch. They sound rather angry . . ."

I called.

It was a Staff Captain, and he was indeed angry. He said: "We can't find your contract anywhere, where the hell is it?"

I said: "Sir, I'm still waiting for you to send it to me for signature."

"What? You haven't had it?"

"No, sir."

"Oh God." He sounded as weary as the rest of us. He said: "A bit awkward—you're supposed to be in Ethiopia."

I remembered that during one of my chats with a cheerful young Lieutenant in his office I'd said: "Find me something in Africa, and I'll sign on again." That had been the second time

I'd lost the papers. I said: "What the hell am I supposed to be doing in Ethiopia?"

I could hear the rustle of papers at the other end. "It says here you're the new Police Commissioner."

"For God's sake, I'm an actor, not a policeman."

The rustling again. "It says here you used to be in the Palestine police."

"I'd forgotten, that was a long time ago. How come I haven't been told about it?"

"Don't ask me, for God's sake. You're supposed to be on your way there. Can you come over to the office and get it all cleared up? One way or another?"

"I'll be over."

Ethiopia . . . I'd been too long with the Eighth Army in North Africa to appreciate the damp and cold of England; nobody had any coal to burn, and I was sleeping in an overcoat.

I went over to the War Office, and they sent me to the Foreign Office, and there they stared at me coldly and gave me a briefing. The Colonel said carefully: "What's your view on the color bar?"

It was still in the days where wogs, they said, began at Dover. I said: "I don't call Negroes niggers, if that's what you mean."

He cheered up at once. "Well, that's admirable. We have a problem out there. The South Africans."

"Oh."

For them, the war had finished much earlier. They were not permitted to leave Africa, so once the Eighth and First Armies had met on the North African coast, sweeping up the last remaining Axis forces, they were all out of work. The Foreign Office, with its customary blandness, had put them to work policing Ethiopia, and that's where the problem began.

There's no one in the world prouder than the Ethiopian. And he's tough; he doesn't take insults lying down. The South

3

Africans were practicing their apartheid on them, and the picture the Colonel painted was not a pretty one.

I said: "A completely free hand?"

He nodded: "Yes, I think so. As long as the mess is cleared up."

"All right. When do you want me to leave?"

He sighed: "According to our records, you're already on the boat to Mombasa. Perhaps you'd better try and find one. The Adjutant will make out the necessary movement order. Do try and get there as soon as you can, won't you?"

Ten days later, I was there.

*   *   *

I had spent the major part of the war in Egypt, Libya, and Tunisia, most of the time behind the lines in the sand-dune country where the Sahara Desert undulates down to the sea. This was my first time in the real Africa—the Africa where the people are black, not brown, where they say *Jambo* instead of *Salaam aleikum;* and in those days, it was still Colonial Africa.

Mombasa is one of the most beautiful harbors on earth, and no one who has been there will ever forget it.

As we steamed into the lovely estuary, the sun was shining on the red tile roofs of the houses that lined the green banks; reds and greens, and the purple of bougainvillea were everywhere. It was hot and humid, but the breeze that blew across the water was cool and refreshing. Above all, the sun was bright, and the sky was clear, a brilliant, almost blinding blue.

It was a fascinating place. It was already a port of some consequence more than six hundred years ago, and the red-stone fortress which stands on its own coral eminence and dominates the approaches to the harbor still contrives to conjure up visions of Vasco da Gama, although it was not built until nearly a hundred years after da Gama's first visit there.

It reeks of the Portuguese wars; there are broken-down castellated walls, now overgrown with creepers, and you cannot enter Fort Jesus itself without thinking of the tiny garrison that held it for three years against the raiders sent by the Immam of Oman in the sixteen-nineties; there were only thirteen defenders left, two of them women, when the city finally surrendered. It looks like a stage setting for Verdi's *Don Carlos*. Today, Fort Jesus is a prison, and there's a certain vicarious delight in the juxtaposition of the two ideas.

The town is a bustling and cheerful place—noisy, dusty, and colorful. Its streets are crowded with tourists, and there are always carpet-sellers at their heels. There are ancient brass-studded doorways everywhere, intricately carved and decorated. The stores are full of Benares brass, Kashmiri wool, filigree work from Aden, lacquered ivory from Iran, carved jade from China, and beaded leatherwork from the interior. You buy coconut milk in the streets, and the vendor will slice the top off the husk for you with his razor-sharp bush knife, exposing a quart or more of the cool liquid. One quick slash, just above a grizzled thumb, and the top is off. These are not the coconuts you find in the Western markets. They are picked before the milk has had time to solidify, and all it really needs is a jigger of vodka or gin.

The ubiquitous and harrassed Transit Officer was on the dock to meet those of us who knew, more or less, where we were going, and I was taken to one of the almost deserted military camps, an empty, sprawling place set in barbed wire among the sand dunes. A few white-robed Wakamba servants were squatting at their washtubs, beaming their bright smiles, pounding their laundry with large round stones, moving rhythmically in the sunlight. I went over to one of them with a pile of accumulated laundry under my arm. He stood up and held out his hands for it.

Swahili, I knew, was closely akin to Arabic, which I spoke

fairly well. I had picked up a Swahili dictionary on the ship and had studied it a little.

I said: "Can I have this by this afternoon?" It was now ten o'clock in the morning.

He nodded, smiling broadly: "At six o'clock, *bwana.*"

It was strange to be called *bwana* instead of *effendi.*

I said: "Six o'clock won't do. By teatime."

"Yes, *bwana.* I will do it now. Six o'clock."

I said patiently: "Too late. I must have it by teatime."

Nodding happily, he agreed: "Six o'clock, *bwana.*"

He repeated the phrase again, *sa'a sitta,* six o'clock, saying it over and over so that if I did not understand it the first time, then I might benefit by its constant repetition.

Then he raised his arm and pointed to the sun. In slow, careful words, like a man explaining to a child, he said: "When the sun is up there, up high."

"Good."

As I turned away, he added: "At six o'clock."

At midday, he brought my laundry back. It was washed, dried, and ironed.

He said proudly: "Six o'clock, *bwana.* Ready."

I nodded and paid him. When he had gone, I called to a white-robed African who was standing nearby, swinging his charcoal iron back and forth in wide sweeps to make the coals inside it glow. I asked him what the time was. Not stopping his rhythmic movements, he looked briefly up at the sun and told me it was six o'clock. I gave up.

The mystery was solved that night when I was dining with one of the nurses from the hospital. She told the waiter to have a taxi ready at midnight; the phrase *sa'a sitta* grated like chalk on a slate.

She'd been there a long time, and her Swahili was fluent. I said: "For God's sake, the Swahili numbers are supposed to be the same as Arabic, where I come from *sa'a sitta* is six o'clock."

6

"So it is in Swahili."

I waited.

She said quickly: "The Africans have a more logical system than we do. One o'clock is the first hour of the day, so six o'clock is six hours after sunrise. Or six hours after sunset. Easy, isn't it?"

"Five in the afternoon?"

"They call it eleven o'clock, daytime."

"And five in the morning?"

"Eleven o'clock, nighttime."

"Isn't that rather complicated?"

"On the contrary."

"Uh-huh."

"You'll find the African always takes the easy way. If he doesn't know the name of a thing, he describes it."

"Pigeon English?"

"Not quite. Onomatopoeia. That's a great word, isn't it?"

"Uh-huh."

"A motorcycle is a *pinka-pinka*. A tractor is a *tonka-tonka*. Bits of Arabic thrown in. You know the Arabic word for pepper?"

"*Filfil.*"

"Here they call it *pili-pili.*" Holding up the bottle of Tabasco sauce, she said: "He doesn't give a damn about where this comes from. He's never heard of Mexico, much less Tabasco. But this stuff is made with pepper, and it burns his mouth."

"So?"

"So, he calls it *pili-pili-ho-ho*. What could be simpler?"

It was my introduction to the uncluttered African mind.

* * *

I took the train to Nairobi, and somehow contrived to pass through the National Park, one of the best-stocked game reserves in the world, without the sight or sound of a wild animal of any kind. I hung out of the window all the way, rubbernecking for lion or leopard or elephant; nothing. Nothing but mile after mile of yellow gray bush, with telephone lines strung across it, the wires down frequently where the giraffe had charged through them. (When this happens, the local tribesmen would hastily gather up the copper wire before the arrival of the repair crews, and fashion it into bracelets for their women.)

The journey was slow and lazy and pleasant, but the wartime circumstances, still prevailing, robbed it of any exotic flavor; my traveling companions were all young army officers, the new breed of late-war conscripts, who seemed excessively soft and unmilitary.

There was no time for more than a brief look at Nairobi.

Its main street was astonishing—wide enough to turn an oxcart around in, and with an air that was altogether European and therefore a little disappointing. A town with no *raison d'être* at all, no river, no port, no junction of highways. It grew there merely because, when they built the railway line from Mombasa to Lake Victoria in the eighteen-eighties, the crews were held up for three years by the attrition of man-eating lions. An incredible four hundred workmen were taken by the Athi River lions in that period, and while they were waiting for something to be done about them, the depot just grew into a town. Now, its population was close to a hundred and twenty thousand.

I was anxious to push on to Ethiopia, and I finally hitched a ride on a convoy that was going north as far as Hargeisa, the capital of British Somaliland.

The convoy was a masterpiece of East African disorganization. It was made up of ten-ton diesels, driven by ex-POWs

(Italians), and it took a week to make the eight-hundred-mile journey through some of the most fearful bush I have ever seen, through the wild deserts of the Northern Frontier Province, over the crocodile-infested Tana River, where fifty panting Africans dragged the trucks on rafts across the broad muddy water, stomping their splayed feet and chanting, on through the barren Jubaland wastes into the more barren Ogaden (skillfully bypassing the pleasant little towns on the Somalia littoral) and into the wide depressing plateau of Somaliland, where the sand is gypsum-sour and the shrubbery is sparse and gray.

Long wooden benches had been set out in the trucks, and I commandeered the rear place on the leading vehicle; I was thinking about the sun, which I like, and had forgotten the dust, which was appalling. It enveloped the whole convoy in a fine red cloud that traveled with us all the way. There was mile after countless mile of fine red sand that blossomed up out of the soil and hung over us as we went, getting into our eyes, our noses, our throats, and our food. Twice a day we stopped for meals, which consisted of corned beef, hard biscuits, and tea—the old Western Desert ration. Every evening at five, we drew the trucks up into a laager and made camp, sleeping in the open on the soft red sand that was everywhere.

In later times I never ceased to wonder at the incredible discomfort of this trip. When I found out, which was soon enough, just how much comfort and luxury the bush has to offer, I was astounded that we had been so acutely miserable on that long and tortured journey.

I was accustomed to the rigors of the Sahara, where you lived just as long as your supplies held out and no longer, but the bush was strange to me. It was not until later, when I came to live on my rifle, that I realized what an abundance of good food there is there—of venison, wild boar, partridge, and guinea fowl. And what great comfort can easily be provided with a minimum of forethought. But the ostrich-egg omelettes and

the kudu steaks came later; so did the cool evenings under the
thorn trees with a bottle of ice-cold beer to help the lethargy
along.

But the journey was over at last. We limped into the big
military camp at Hargeisa and I sank down tired and dirty on
the camp cot that was waiting for me in a tiny, bare, whitewashed room.

The inevitable African servant came in, inevitably beaming,
and handed me a small bowl of water, about enough to weaken
a decent-sized whisky.

I said sourly: "What the hell's that supposed to be for?"

He said happily: "Water ration, *bwana.*"

I stormed into the Adjutant's office, a big tent set out on a
torn green tarpaulin.

I said: "What the devil's all this nonsense about a water
ration?"

He was quite hostile about it. He said tartly: "Well, I'm
sorry, but we're practically out of water just now. The rain's not
due for another month yet."

"In the middle of the damned Sahara Desert, I never went
without enough water."

"That's very interesting. But here, the ration is half a gallon
per man per day for ablutions."

"Do you mean for washing?"

He looked at me coldly. "For ablutions. Anyway, aren't you
the fellow from the Foreign Office?"

"Yes. I'm on my way to Dire-Daua."

"Then you're nothing to do with me at all."

"How am I supposed to get there?"

"I haven't the vaguest idea."

"Then let me see the Brigadier."

"He's out hunting."

"The Colonel will do."

"I'm afraid he's on the tennis courts."

"Tennis? In this dump?"

"We have an excellent court."

"Who looks after transport?"

"I do."

"Then can I have a truck?"

He said: "And we're terribly short of petrol too. Besides, I don't really see why I should have to worry about your movements, you're only quasi-military now, you know . . ."

I interrupted him: "Can I have either a truck, or access to your radio, to tell them in London that I can't get any farther because of the stupidity of the camp personnel?"

He looked at me distastefully for a moment, wondering if he should find a few more objections. I outranked him, and was not in the best of tempers. He decided it wouldn't be worth while. He reached for his pen.

"I'll give you a movement order. But the vehicle can only go . . ."

"You mean the truck."

"The vehicle can only go as far as the Ethiopian border. We're not allowed into the Reserved Areas without the express consent of the Commissioner of Police there."

"Well, that's nice to know, anyway."

"I beg your pardon?"

"I am the Commissioner."

He blinked at me. "The Commissioner is a man called Calogreedy, a South African. My information is that you're being posted to him."

"Then your information's way out of kilter. I'm taking over from him."

He stared at me blankly for a moment. "Oh. Oh, I see." He was smiling suddenly. He said: "Well, of course, in that case . . . But our vehicles are very definitely prohibited from entering Ethiopia without the express consent of the Brigadier, and he's not here now. But as far as the border, yes, of course. Would you care for a brandy and soda? That's quite a tiring trip up from Nairobi, isn't it?"

I discovered the reason for his change of tone when we were on our way out of the camp. I said to the Sergeant who was driving the truck along the gritty road that led across the plain, the dust billowing out in a long plume behind us: "Do you get up to Dire-Daua very often?"

"No, sir. Bit hard to get a permit. They don't like us up there. We're the Military over the border standing by in case of trouble. They have a civilian administration, and they're very touchy about that sort of thing."

"Civilian? It's run by army officers."

He nodded. He was a careerman, thirty years in the army and as hard as nails. He said: "That's right, sir. But they're responsible to the Foreign Office, not the War Office. Makes them feel like they've put one over on us. Come to that, they probably have. We have to get a dozen permits if we want to go there."

"Anything there worth going for?"

He looked at me in astonishment, and said pleasantly: "This must be your first time out here, sir?"

The truck was bouncing like a wild horse over the dirt track. A single umbrella thorn stood out against the hot sky, and as far as you could see there was nothing else but flat gray rock and flat brown sand. He pointed; a herd of wild boar were moving slowly across our front.

He said: "Dire-Daua, what a place." He sighed. "It's on the other side of the Madar Pass, where the good soil is. Down here, nothing but desert, look at it, enough to make a grown man weep. But there . . . different as chalk from cheese. It's green and . . . civilized. The local Paris."

"Well, that's nice to know."

"Girls, music, cafés, hotels, cinemas . . . All we've got in Hargeisa is the NAAFI and a couple of leftover nurses. Leftovers from the Eighth Army. You ought to see them."

"I know. When they first sent nurses to the Western Desert, there was a rule about them. Nobody under forty. Unofficially, they were screened in London and Cairo before they went there. Anybody who looked worth raping was sent back home again. Bad for the troops' morale, they said."

The Sergeant laughed happily. "That's about the size of it in Hargeisa. That dried-up riverbed we've got isn't wet enough to be called the arse-hole of Africa, but if it was, then we'd be a two hundred miles up it."

"The army has a special talent for inhabiting uninhabitable places."

"That's why we all like to get to Dire-Daua when we can." He looked at me sideways. "I'm supposed to drop you at the border, sir. How will you manage then?"

"How far from the border to the nearest police post?"

"Forty miles, at Jig-Jigga. There's a police station there. Big market town."

"Well, there's presumably a frontier post of some sort. Won't they have transport?"

He was grinning broadly. "The post is only manned in daylight. After dark, they all go home. Like I said, civilized."

"So take me on to Jig-Jigga. We'll worry about it when we get there."

He settled himself more comfortably in his seat, and brushed the sweat off the back of his neck.

*　*　*

I did not think it wise to stop long in Jig-Jigga. We pulled up at the police station and I went inside. There was an Ethiopian orderly on duty. I asked: "Is one of the officers available?".

He looked at me and shook his head. Then he said quickly: "Italiano? Français? Deutsch?"

In the three years of occupation the Italians had done a great deal to Ethiopia. Their record there was not a good one, but they had built roads, telegraph systems, railways . . . And they had imposed their language on the people by the simple expedient of refusing to deal with them in Amharic, so that every Tom, Dick, and Harry, even in the bush, knew at least a smattering of Italian. They have a great talent for learning. I was to find out that in the towns, they often spoke it very well.

I asked the orderly if he really spoke three European languages.

"Under the Italians," he said, "I learn Italian. In school, French. After that, German, in the Mission."

"Mission?"

"Mission school, sir. But no good."

"Oh? Why not?"

He was faintly embarrassed. "No drinking," he said. "No smoking. No women. Not good for a man."

I got back to the matter in hand. "Do you have a radio station here?"

"Yes, sir."

"Have them send this message to the Brigadier in Hargeisa."

I wrote on a sheet of paper: "Request permission to take your truck and driver on to Dire-Daua. No police transport available here."

I complimented the policeman on his smart appearance, and told him to send the Brigadier's answer on to Dire-Daua. He stood rigidly to attention until I left.

Three hours later, we were in Dire-Daua.

14

2

The road came to a dead end after a steep and winding descent from the Harar escarpment. All the way down from the high mountain the cliff had been falling sharply into the bottom of the gorge, first on one side, then on the other. The road was still in good condition, a tarmac road put down by the Italians in their march to the capital.

The deep black of the cool night, mysterious and exciting, was relieved from time to time by tiny sparks of fire in the distance, where here and there, scattered at random on the slopes of the rugged mountain, kerosene pressure lamps were lighting up some minuscule compound, a thorn tree *zeriba* surrounding a round adobe hut called a *tukul,* the long sharp spikes of the fence keeping the prowling animals out. I could hear the bleating of goats. On each side, the mountain fell away fast into the darkness of the chasm.

Then the moon came up, and the horizon seemed thousands of miles away, a limitless vista of purple and gray that stretched out into cold infinity. The jagged, startling rocks were all around us, and the air was ripe with the rich scent of honey-suckle.

At the bottom of the hill, a simple knife rest of barbed wire and wood was swung open for us by a sleepy sentry who flashed a light in our faces and grunted, and then let us through without comment. I told the driver to drop me at the hotel.

"Which one, sir? There are three good ones."

"The one that has the best bar."

He grinned and swung the truck round in a wide circle. A few minutes later, we found ourselves in the wide tropical garden of the C.I.A.A.O. Hotel, where bright flowers were growing, strangely luminescent in the moonlight, and heavily scented. There was red hibiscus flowering side by side with the white velvet *frangi-pani* whose sweet and potent smell always seems to remind the traveler that he is home again, back in the serene peacefulness of Africa after the savage concrete beehive of his European cities, where the farthest horizon is across the other side of a wet and noisy street.

After the driver had gone happily about his business—I saw him later that night with a girl on his arm—I sat in the dim-lit lounge of the hotel and had some *tej*, which is the national drink in Ethiopia. It is made from fermented honey, rather in the fashion of the old Saxon mead, and ranges in quality from the Royal *tej* which is brewed for the Emperor, and is as smooth and mellow as good sherry, to the cloudy white liquid sold in the market squares at a few pennies a beer-bottleful. They say it is an acquired taste; I acquired a taste for it there and then in the high, faintly illuminated foyer of the C.I.A.A.O. Hotel.

It was almost deserted. An Italian barman was slowly, methodically, absently polishing glasses behind an ornate bamboo counter. Someone was snoring in a rattan armchair under a thick cluster of fronds. Two girls, who looked like Armenians, were whispering in a corner with a slight, well-dressed man who affected a monocle and a long cigarette holder. He was speaking French with a strong Central European accent, and when he turned to look at me I saw with surprise that the monocle was made of opaque glass, and I wondered about it. An Italian-looking woman was reading a novel under the shaded light of a modernistic lamp; she looked up once or twice and stared at me when she thought I wasn't looking, and turned hastily away again when she saw that her reflection in the mirror over the bar was in my full sight. She had long, loose blonde hair, rather untidy, and a full, overdeveloped figure. She was quite attractive, but the lines round her mouth were hard and her eyes were cold. I wondered why she was alone, and almost began to speak with her, then changed my mind. The barman came over to replenish my glass.

I asked him: "What sort of a place is this?"

He shrugged: "Fine. As long as you don't break a leg."

"No doctors?"

"There is one at the camp, *signore.*"

"The camp?"

"A company of the King's African Rifles. They have a camp here, over on the old airfield."

"The army? I thought they weren't allowed in Dire-Daua?"

He shrugged. "A standby company in case of trouble. They don't do any harm." He smiled. "You must be the new Police Commissioner?"

"Yes, I am. How did you know?"

He shrugged. "A small town, *signore.* Everybody knows everybody else's business. Bazaar gossip."

17

I said: "How come the doctor in the camp can't set a broken leg?"

He nodded toward a corner of the lounge. Half obscured by greenery which hung from every rafter, a tall young Lieutenant of the King's African Rifles was lolling in an armchair in a music-hall drunken pose. He was snoring loudly, and nursing an empty beer bottle, lovingly.

I was surprised that an Italian bartender should have survived here, and I said: "Do they give you a bad time, the local people?"

The Italian-Ethiopian war had been brutal, and had left a lot of scars. The Ethiopian guerrillas, some of the most fearless (and dangerous) fighters in the world, had a way with their prisoners. They would tie them to a tree, stripped naked, cut a thin line across the belly with the point of a dagger, and pull off the skin all the way down to the knees; it was a point of honor among them to get the genitals off in one piece. The guerrillas had been fighting with spears and knives against aircraft and tanks, and had still contrived to give the occupying armies of Marshal Graziani a very bad time indeed.

But he was smiling again. "No, *signore*, not any more. I was Mess Orderly for Prince Amedeo, the Duke of Aosta, not really a soldier." He said again, disassociating himself from any thought of war: "Just a Mess Orderly, but a good one."

I finished my drink and went to look at the town.

In the cool freshness of the evening, it was a pretty little place, consisting largely of one street which ran from the police HQ to the railway station, a road which crossed it running from nowhere to nowhere, and a few obscure streets in between. But it was bright and well lit; there were two or three hotels, all with pavement terraces, and a good many cafés at which an odd mixture of Greeks, Armenians, French, Italians, Poles, Czechs, and Ethiopians sat around in a leisurely fashion, arguing, talking, gesticulating, sipping aperitifs; sometimes they stopped as

I went past to look at me with that oddly speculative appraisal, not quite surreptitious and not quite overt. I was very conscious that they knew who I was and were waiting to see what was going to happen now.

In a small provincial town that goes its own way without outside interference, a change in the police administration can open the place right up—or close it right down. The authority of an occupying exarch can be very arbitrary, and I knew what they were asking each other: Was I going to make myself a nuisance?

There would be other questions too. Were the liquor laws —if any—going to be enforced? Would there be a clampdown on the smuggling that went on? Would all the brothels be closed in accordance with the known British stuffiness? Did I play poker? Could I hold my drink? For them, it was all a matter of some consequence.

The little town, lost in the empty immensity of the African mountains, no more than a pinprick on a vast sand table, as far away as the moon from all I had ever known, was astonishingly European in character, but European in a very old-world sense. Even though the majority of the people on the streets were Ethiopian, striding with great dignity even when they were aimlessly wandering, the flavor was still, as the Sergeant had said, of Paris, with a touch of the Italian resorts thrown in for good measure. There were advertisements for Cinzano everywhere, and Marie Brizard, and Gomme Pirelli, and Parfums Lanvin, and all the nostalgic products that seemed to reflect a prewar Europe, where people sat in pavement cafés, just as they did here, and played chess as they watched the world go by.

And then, I collided accidentally with a white-haired old gentleman dressed in white jodhpurs and an army blanket, and the image was gone. He made a courtly little bow, and raised a battered topee in a gesture that seemed to come out of the

19

best of Edwardian England. I wished I knew how to say "I beg your pardon" in Amharic, but I didn't; so I merely raised my hands apologetically, and he smiled and said: *"Te'ena ysterling, God be with you,"* and went on his way with the unruffled dignity of a king.

There was a cacophony of European languages coming from the terraces. A cinema poster was advertising *Le Jour Se Leve,* with Jean Gabin and Arletty. The Ethiopian girls who wandered in pairs along the road were dressed in bright-flowered cotton dresses, not cut in the shapeless Mother Hubbard style of the East Africans, but carefully, even fashionably made. Some of them were quite remarkably beautiful, by any standard —high cheekbones, large black eyes with a lively gleam to them, coffee-colored skins that shone in the lamplight, wiry hair piled high in concentric rings, and a tendency to giggle as they passed by.

I found a dark, dusty street that seemed to lead to nowhere, and wandered down it. Broken stone walls, whitewashed adobe huts, a cow lying asleep on what was once a sidewalk . . . There were tin roofs here, an open water trough, a pile of freshly cut ironwood poles. A woman was breast-feeding a baby, seated on the front step of a small house, and eating a mango.

Farther on, the houses disappeared altogether, and there was open, rugged ground that sloped down to a dry riverbed, and on its edge there was a barricade of coiled barbed wire. Across on the other bank, I could see more houses, closely packed together, and lit, not as they were on this side with electric lights, but with kerosene lamps. I followed the fence for a while, stumbling in the soft sand of the river's bottom, and came to a wooden knife rest, a policeman sitting idly by it, and when I approached he sprang to attention and saluted. For a moment, he just stood there as I looked at the barricade and the houses beyond it, and he said softly: *"Proibito, signore,"* He added: "The Magallo."

I nodded and turned away, heading back toward the little main street. I found the railway station at one end of it, a rambling, low-built pile of yellow bricks, all locked up for the night now, and I turned back to where the bright lights were. The crowds were coming out of the movie houses, noisy, cheerful, crowding the street, shouting to each other and laughing. Some of them were smartly dressed in white *shammas* and sandals, carrying their inevitable walking sticks and moving with the oddly regal step of the Amhara. Some were in rags, some in hot-country European clothes. I heard snatches of conversation in a dozen languages and as many different dialects.

The smell of strong coffee tempted me, and I climbed the steps to a terraced coffee shop that was half-hidden from the street by a wall of brilliant creeping vines, and sat at a red-checkered table and ordered beer and coffee. The coffee was strong, strong as it is in Turkey or Egypt, with a strangely bitter tang to it; Harar coffee, one of the best in the world.

It occurred to me that coffee was supposed by some to have taken its name from the Ethiopian town of Kaffa; a legend said that a goatherd noticed that his flock was getting high on the berries they were eating and tried chewing them himself; he got high too, and coffee was born. Apocryphal, perhaps, but the kind of story from which history is fashioned. The beer was good too, and served in glasses that had been sensibly kept on ice; the night was hot.

Close by, a very black man was sitting with an attractive young woman, and I saw that he was watching me from time to time. I was to learn later that the "correct" color in Ethiopia is a deep brown, that black skin is considered a social disadvantage because it is the color of the slaves who traditionally were brought from the south and the southwest, the historic slave centers of Kenya, Uganda, and the Congo. He was dressed in a very smart gray wool suit that could only have come from

London, and he was chatting idly with his girl in beautiful, if rather poetic, Italian. I heard him say to her: "Well, we'd better get back to the palace. If we can get that damned car started . . ."

As he left with her, he passed my table and stopped and smiled. He said: "I've an idea that you're the new Police Commissioner, am I right?"

I stood up and looked at the girl, but he did not introduce her. I said: "Not quite yet. I will be."

"When you are, we'll meet officially." His English was faultless, straight out of Oxford. He shot out his hand and said: "I'm the Duke of Harar. You'll no doubt hear lots about me, most of it bad."

He was laughing suddenly, a charming, delightful young man of twenty-eight or thirty, and then he was taking her arm and was gone.

It was the briefest of all encounters, but somehow it left me with an indefinable feeling of pleasure. All my life, my pleasures, my sadness, my hatreds, my loves, have all been derived from trivia; somehow, I just felt good.

I finished my third beer and had a Pernod for a nightcap, then wandered off again into the town, getting my bearings, learning the indefinable feel of the place, letting its character seep in with the warm night air, breathing in its mood and its temper. In the morning, I knew, it would be different, with the heat of the day and the bustle of work; but this was the time to get to know the nature of my new home, when its people were relaxed and its arms were open. In the morning, I knew, I would be a stranger, a newcomer, even an intruder perhaps; but now, I was part of the town that was to be my headquarters for the next two years.

The lights were dying out one by one. The waiters were hurriedly sweeping the pavements clean. The young girls had all gone home to their beds. I went back to the hotel and slept till daylight.

At ten o'clock the next morning, I went round to police headquarters and reported for duty. Under the circumstances, I was not expecting a very affable reception; I was not disappointed.

The South African Commissioner glared at me and said: "What the hell were you doing wandering around the town last night? Why didn't you report to me at once?"

He was a dark, athletic-looking man, brown as the people who had given Ethiopia—Land of the Sunburned Faces—its name; a large black moustache gave him the look of a Barbary pirate. He was a handsome man, but not in too good a temper. He shuffled papers on his desk, sucked noisily on his pipe, and said: "His Excellency the Governor is waiting to see you at the residence, you'd better get over there. And hurry."

* * *

I had heard in London of the Governor. He was quite a legend.

Brigadier General Sir Reginald Smith, sixty-three years old, with forty years of service in Somaliland behind him.

In those days, it was customary for the English civil servants to spend eighteen months in these dreary outposts—and Somaliland is the dreariest of them all—and then to take six months' leave back in England. On occasion, two terms are spent in the field, and the leave accumulates to a year; it's a very solid way to live, the sharp contrast between service and vacation providing a marked and stimulating contrast.

But Sir Reginald—he was plain Reggie Smith in those days—had served out four terms in the desert, a total of six years, without any leave at all. He just let the time slip by whenever he was due for a holiday, and simply sent a cable to the Colonial Office in London saying he'd defer again. At the end of six years, he was *ordered* to take his leave. He refused. They sent out a replacement for him, with written orders to get on board that ship and take his holiday.

For a while he complained that the Somaliland desert had become his home, that all he loved or was interested in was there. But the orders were firm, and the ship was waiting. He was *escorted* down to Berbera, one hundred and twenty miles from his HQ in Hargeisa, and put aboard the Orient Line steamer that was on its way to London.

He made it as far as Aden—the next one hundred miles. There, he disembarked, took an Arab dhow back to Berbera, and spent his two years' accumulated leave in this tiny, dusty, barren fishing village.

He spoke Somali, a difficult language that has no written form, with remarkable ease and accuracy. He knew the histories of the various warring tribes—all Somali tribes are mutually hostile—and knew their leaders, their Sheikhs, and their *Khadis*, or Holy Men. He knew every inch of its sixty-eight thousand square miles of empty bush, dotted here and there with camel scrub, with dry rivers that became torrents in the brief and wasted rains, though the average rainfall is only one inch or less a year.

It is somehow symptomatic of Somaliland that its population is an estimated six hundred and fifty thousand, and that its herds of camels number over a million, its sheep three million, and its goats two million—or roughly ten animals and a tenth of a square mile of territory for every man, woman, and child in the country. You can travel the whole of its two-hundred-mile length from east to west—and it takes at least four days in a good truck—without seeing more than a single solitary nomad, standing on one leg in the characteristic pose, leaning on his stick and watching over his beloved camels, which are the whole raison d'être of a Somali's existence.

In this empty desolation, the present Governor of the Reserved Areas of Ethiopia had spent all his adult life. Not even during his army career had he left the territories of the Somali tribes. The rest of Africa hated and distrusted them, but to him they were blood brothers; he admired them with a passionate devotion.

And I was aware that no one in Africa disliked them more than the Ethiopians he had now come to govern; there was a mutual distrust between the two peoples that bordered on paranoia.

It promised a very interesting situation.

3

The Governor lived in a large, rambling, stone-built house that had once been the residence of the Italian administrator. It was dark and sombre, with a white-stone wall around its small and dark green garden, and was shaded from the morning sun by bright purple bougainvillea and rampant honeysuckle. As I walked up the short driveway of flagstone interspersed with a yellow green weed, I saw a woman on the veranda, a Somali by the looks of her, gather up some beadwork and hurry away; "scuttle away" was the phrase that came to mind.

He was a big man, Sir Reginald, bluff and well built, the kind of man you would normally call "hearty." But his quick smile was shy and nervous, and his eyes had that benign, placatory look to them that is more easily associated with Santa Claus than with a military Governor. He was simply dressed in khaki shorts and shirt, the red tabs and badges of rank on the collar.

A Somali servant, a thin young man in the traditional white gown and fez, showed me to the veranda where he was waiting, and he took my hand warmly and said: "We've met before, haven't we?"

Indeed we had. I had met him, very briefly, in Nairobi; at that time, I did not know who he was. His voice was quiet, almost a whisper, and he seemed hopelessly ill at ease.

I said: "I'm afraid I'm interrupting something, sir?"

He was aghast. "No, no, not at all. Would you like a drink? What about a Black Velvet? We have a lot to talk about."

He was bustling about as though he didn't quite know what to do, and I was to discover later that he felt quite out of place whenever the slightest coloring of protocol was in the air. For far too long he had lived in barren spaces where there just weren't any other Englishmen around; and he simply didn't know what should be done. He was anxious, nonetheless, to make me feel comfortable. He waved a vague hand at nothing in particular, and said: "I'm really not used to all this . . . this formality. It's strange to live in a house that has plumbing."

The furniture was rough and practical, hand-hewn chairs cut from thorn-tree wood and covered over with locally cured hides, still haired and smelling slightly of the fish oil the coastal Somalis use for tanning. There were two or three beautiful Somali shawls hanging on the walls, and a great deal of the ornamental beadwork of the interior.

He said, searching for easy conversation, pointing at the beaded aprons: "The Issa Mahmoud tribe . . . the Hassan Mahmouds . . . the Isshaks . . . Some of them are really quite valuable."

I thought then—and still do—that the Governor was one of the nicest men I had ever met; we were to become close and good friends.

The young Somali servant brought champagne and Guinness, and mixed it in cold pewter tankards, and we toasted each other and sat down to talk.

He said, smiling nervously: "I imagine you've met the present Commissioner?"

"Yes, I have. I hope he won't be staying too long?"

"As soon as you're ready to take over from him."

"I'm ready now."

Again, that quick, nervous smile. "Yes, of course. Well, perhaps in a few days. You ought to take a look at the territory first, if you'd like to do that?"

I said: "I studied the maps in London. It seemed to me that nobody knew where the boundaries were."

He said carefully: "Yes, yes, I suppose they are a little bit uncertain, but . . . Well, for the moment Ethiopia is divided into two parts. First, there's the Emperor's undisputed territory which the British army took from the Italians and very properly handed back to him, and then there are all the disputed areas which the Somalis, or the French, or the Danakil are claiming as theirs. The borders never were very well defined in this part of the world, and I'm afraid that once the Italians got chased out, everybody moved into the vacuum and said *this is mine*. That's why we're holding it, until proper ownership can be decided by the United Nations. The Reserved Areas, which we govern, comprise the whole of the Ogaden, which is—oh, about sixty or seventy thousand square miles, I'd say, plus the railway line and the land around it, all the way from the French Somaliland border up to Addis Ababa, plus the European conclave of Dire-Daua. It's all fairly well defined, if not physically, at least in our own minds. We know, more or less, roughly where the borders are."

I said: "The railway from the border to Addis, that must be about five hundred miles?"

"Four hundred and fifty."

"And how far on each side of it is that undefined border?"

He took a long drink of his Black Velvet. "Twenty feet on each side." If it seemed incongruous to him, he gave no sign of it. As an old professional army man, he was not the type to criticize the Establishment in London, or to doubt their wisdom.

But the inference was astonishing. I said, trying not to sound too surprised: "So we have, virtually, a distinct and separately governed country which is four hundred and fifty miles long and only forty feet wide."

He corrected me: "Not a country. A Reserved Area. And we have the whole of the Ogaden . . ." He broke off and said: "That's about the size of the whole of England, isn't it? And Dire-Daua, which I'm sure you're going to like very much, a delightful place."

"But not the *whole* of Dire-Daua."

"No. The Old Town." He smiled. "I suppose you could call it the native quarter, that belongs to *them*. We don't ever go into it. It's called the Magallo."

"Where the barbed-wire barriers are."

"Ah yes, of course, you were down in the riverbed last night, weren't you? The Commissioner told me. I'm afraid he was very angry with you."

"Yes, I rather gathered that. I take it the railway station in Addis Ababa is ours, but not the rest of the town?"

"And twenty feet around it."

"I would imagine that there must be a few administrative problems involved."

"Er, well, yes, I suppose there are. We try and avoid them. London is very anxious that we shouldn't rock the boat too much."

I said, thinking it was time to change the subject: "The new British officers for the police are arriving already, I understand. How long before the last of the South Africans goes?"

"That will be the Commissioner himself. As I said, as soon as you're ready."

"Well, suppose I take the train up to Addis Ababa and look around up there for a while."

"But you mustn't leave the area of the railway station."

"I understand. And then visit the rest of the territory by truck? Just drive around the borders of the Ogaden, and get to know where everything is? How long would that take?"

He shook his head. "It would take forever. All you really need to inspect is the only town in the Ogaden, Jig-Jigga. Technically, it's the capital. Actually, the only town there is. Big marketplace. Somalis, of course, just a relatively few Ethiopians. But then, the whole of the Ogaden is Somali."

I thought we should bring it out into the open right away. I said: "Isn't that what all the fuss is about? Don't the Ethiopians say the Ogaden is Ethiopan?"

"Ah yes, yes of course. Do have some more Guinness. I get it from Djibuti, you really must go down there as soon as you get a chance, delightful place, very hot. Plenty of water, but you can't take a shower during the day because the water is piped in over the desert, and it comes out of the taps in steam. You have to wait till well after dark, when it's had a chance to cool off."

He felt it was time to change the subject too.

I said: "What about our relations with the Ethiopians here? If they claim the territory, and we're keeping it from them . . . doesn't that raise problems?"

"Oh no, not in the least. They know they'll get it back sooner or later."

"The Ogaden too?"

He blinked at me and said: "Well, I suppose all that will be decided in London, wouldn't you say?"

"Yes, of course. I'll have to learn Amharic. Can I find a teacher here?"

He thought about it for a while, and said at last: "You'll find two things. First of all, Amharic is probably the most difficult language in the world, and secondly, almost everybody speaks quite good Italian, which I'm told you speak very well."

"Well enough. I'll take a crack at Amharic too, if only as a matter of policy."

"You'll find it quite impossible to learn. Seventy-two letters in the alphabet, I believe, and they all change their forms on the slightest pretext. Have you seen your house?"

"No, sir, not yet."

"I'll send someone round with you, show you where it is. The present Commissioner's been sleeping in the barracks, I can't possibly think why, so it's unoccupied at the moment, and you may as well take it over now. If there's anything you need to fix it up, just let me know. I'm sure you'll be very comfortable there. Are you married?"

"Yes, I am."

"But you won't be bringing your wife out here, I don't imagine?"

Somehow, it surprised me. From what I'd seen of it, Dire-Daua was one of the most delightful little towns I would ever stay in.

I said: "Well, if I have your permission, yes, I thought I would bring her out later on."

"I see." He was very nervous again, preoccupied with his own private thoughts. And it was not until the following day, when we were dining at his house, that I discovered the reason.

There was something on his mind, and he wanted to slough it off. He said, fiddling with a glass of cognac: "I suppose you'll have to know, you're going to find out one way or another. I have a . . . well, a Somali woman living with me. I'm afraid it's rather frowned upon in the service. Does it offend you?"

I said: "My God no. First of all, I already knew that, they told me in London. A trifle disapprovingly."

31

"Oh my God." He was shocked. "Oh my God, that's terrible."

I suppose the feeling is disappearing today, but in the old days of the Colonies, even the most tolerant parts of the Empire, the Establishment just didn't sleep with black women. It was considered a terrible way to behave. Enlightenment had not yet overtaken us out there.

I said: "I really believe that times are changing, you know. You've been out of touch for a long time, haven't you?"

"Yes, I suppose I have. When I was a young man, in Somalia, they were very stern about it. They told me you just never take a black girl to your bed. Only thing is—well, after thirty years, they tend to look a little whiter."

"I'm sure nobody minds any more."

"You don't?"

"No, of course not. None of my damn business anyway."

Then it came out. "But I'm sure your wife would be very upset about it. I'd have to keep it terribly secret."

"And that's not true either. She's not really an army wife, you know."

The army wife, in those days, was a breed apart. In the outposts, the distant stations in the forests and deserts of Africa, it was the British army wife who kept, with a fanatical determination, to the characteristic foibles that have made the colonial Englishman a caricature the world over. It was she who demanded that he dress for dinner in the middle of the jungle; it was she who held, against all comers, to the feverish fancies of English country life; and it was she who upheld, with militant determination, all the little niceties of Victorian society.

I said: "My wife was as thoroughly out of place in the army as I was."

He still wasn't quite convinced. I could almost see the old prohibitions falling apart and being hastily erected again, but

32

he said at last, quite suddenly: "I wonder if I should . . . if I should introduce you?"

"Well, I'm going to meet her sooner or later, surely?"

"Yes. Yes, of course." He was beaming, flushed with genuine pleasure, with all the charming delight of a small boy. He spoke to the servant in Somali, and almost at once, Armina appeared.

She must have been twenty-six years old, a big, heavily built woman, with the kind of features that suggested she had once been very attractive, with the large Somali eyes and the smooth honey-skin that was so highly prized by the slavers and the sultans. Her breasts under the colorful cotton print dress were heavy, and her hips were huge. But she was smiling brightly when she took my hand, and she said in broken Italian: "I don't speak English, but my Italian is very good, no? So we will be very good friends, very good friends indeed."

Catching the trend of the conversation, the Governor said: "We talk Somali, of course, and she doesn't understand a word of English, so let me tell you at once, she's very hurt because I felt I had to banish her to the kitchen while you were here. Now that's all right, isn't it?"

"Yes, everything's all right now."

I found it odd that a man with his present authority should be concerned over the matter; but he was, and that's all there is to it.

He said, smiling broadly: "She's been with me for fourteen years now, and she's not as young as she used to be, nor as good-looking, but we're very fond of each other."

Fourteen years? She would have been about twelve years old, then, when he first took her, the nubile age at which the desert Somali girls are ready for marriage. Now she was big and clumsy and no longer particularly beautiful.

But I felt at once that she was a woman to be reckoned with.

33

*   *   *

As had been arranged, I spent the next few days in extended tours of the strange, bulbous ribbon of territory which was ours. I took the fast Diesel train to Addis Ababa and down to the French Somaliland border at Douanle, hanging out of the window and watching the varied panorama of desert and mountain, of barren sand and raging torrential rivers, of flat, unhealthy-looking camel scrub and forested peaks of blue granite, staring out at four hundred and fifty miles of the most multiform scenery in the world. The change from desert to high plateau was startling, full of interest, and exciting.

I took an old wartime truck—an Italian Lancia Diesel—and drove it all over the disputed Ogaden, among the wandering tribes of nomads and *shifta*—the bandits who make their living by preying on the caravans that pass through their inhospitable desert.

I spent a few days in the huge market town of Jig-Jigga, where Somalis, Ethiopians, Galla, Danakils, and a dozen other ethnic groups put aside their mutual hatreds in the cause of trade.

And, ten days later, when I arrived back in Dire-Daua, the last of the old regime had gone, and the smiling, chubby, and highly efficient Indian Chief Clerk was ready to hand over to me the administration of the Ethiopian Reserved Areas Police.

4

It was obvious from the start that normal methods of police control—even if I had been versed in them, which I was not —were not going to work under the peculiar circumstances in which we found ourselves. I made up my mind from the beginning that I was going to ignore that long ribbon of railway land as much as possible, and worry only about the town of Dire-Daua, the township of Jig-Jigga, and the Ogaden itself. As for Addis Ababa, it was clear that the Superintendent up there was being merely tolerated, quite good-naturedly, as long as he kept to the railway buildings, but that if he left the line and went into the town itself, he was going to be promptly arrested.

And the Emperor's police, at that time, were officered by ex-British army officers, under a certain Colonel Banks. I made up my mind to go and see him as soon as possible, if only to pay a courtesy call and see if I were going to be arrested too.

But an interesting and exciting incident cleared the way for me. A thief broke in to one of the railway warehouses in Addis Ababa, got thoroughly drunk on looted whisky, and was found there the next morning and handed over to "our" policeman. This in itself was surprising; there was, of course, a certain amount of crime at the station (the warehouses were guarded with a tempting paucity of effort), but in usual circumstances the thief merely had to run twenty feet and he was safe—safe from us because we could not pursuade him into "their" territory, and safe from them because the crime had been committed out of "their" jurisdiction. The actual capture of a criminal there was a very rare event indeed.

I came into the office one morning, and found one of the Superintendents, Bob Howard, waiting for me with a signal in his hand. It had come from our Superintendent in Addis Ababa. It read:

HAVE ARRESTED SO-AND-SO ON CHARGES OF BREAKING AND ENTERING. PLEASE SEND ESCORT.

I said: "What do we usually do in cases like this?"

Bob scratched his head; it was a habit he was rather prone to. He was a good-looking young man of twenty-five or so, not too bright, but a nice fellow of the clean-cut, well-brought-up variety. He had been the first of the new officers to arrive, and as an ex-cop, an expert, he carried a certain amount of authority, merely because he was the only one among us who knew anything at all about police work. He spent most of his time searching through the old files of our predecessors, learning how things ought not to be done; it was the only schooling we ever had.

He said, skimming through pages: "It says here we're supposed to send an Ethiopian officer and a Sergeant to bring the prisoner down here for trial."

"Wouldn't it be easier to hand him over to the Addis Ababa police for action?"

He shrugged his shoulders. "I imagine so. But we're supposed to deal with these cases ourselves. Something about asserting our authority."

"Has it happened before?"

"Only once. They've only caught a thief up there once before, apparently."

"And we sent an escort up for him?"

"Yes, sir."

"What about the witnesses?"

"We brought them down here, too, sir."

"And the Superintendent?"

"Yes, of course. He prosecuted."

"And who looked after the post in his absence?"

"Well . . . I don't know, sir. The Sergeant, I suppose."

"Wouldn't it be easier to kick the offender's backside and let him go?"

"It says here that we're supposed to bring him down here for trial, sir."

"And what allocation do we charge the fares to?"

He flipped some more pages: "Well . . . I think it came out of transport, last time."

The transport allocation in the budget was just about empty, and I said: "No wonder we can't afford spare parts for the trucks. All right, send someone up. Send Inspector Dengel."

The Inspector, traveling alone, left that day, and I forgot all about the matter. The trip up the line took a day and a half, and I expected the prisoner in about three days' time. But it was nearly a week before the sequel came.

Bob came into my office, scratching his head again and

looking very worried. The Ethiopian Adjutant was with him,
looking studiously nonchalant. Their news was brief and to the
point: The train down from Addis had been raided by guerrillas, the prisoner had been taken off and freed, and our Inspector had been put down a dried-up well.

Startled, I said: "Down a well?"

The Adjutant explained gently. He said, in beautiful English: "I am afraid, sir, that the prisoner was a cousin of the
local chieftain at Baroda, a man whose name is Ras Matara."
Looking at the floor, he said: "Your predecessor always called
him a bandit, but it's not really as simple as that. He just
doesn't respect the Emperor's authority over his territory, nor
our jurisdiction over the railway line, which runs through it."

I said: "Good God, bandits on the railway line? Isn't that a
little old-fashioned?"

"We are an old-fashioned people, Commissioner. And the
status quo is so often unsatisfactory, isn't it?"

I was aware that he was making a gentle jibe; the Ethiopians
we employed were working for us willingly, but employment by
an exarchy could not really have been very satisfactory for
them, either. But his smile was all sympathy for my problems,
not his.

I liked talking with him; he was a good man.

He said: "Ras Matara has raided the train, released the
prisoner, and put Inspector Dengel down a dried-up well to
teach him a lesson. I think he will stay there until we go and
get him out."

"By force of arms? His Excellency would have a fit. That's
just the kind of thing we're supposed to avoid."

The Adjutant said gently: "I think a small present . . .
perhaps even a courtesy visit . . ."

"I see. Just how unpleasant is it down a dried-up well?"

He smiled: "Like any other prison. They will drop food and

water down to him from time to time. I do not think they will hurt him."

"Any casualties in the raid on the train?"

"No, sir, nothing. When the train pulled in at the station, Ras Matara simply held it there until his work was done. Inspector Dengel would have sense enough not to resist."

"And the train guards, wouldn't they object?"

He was faintly embarrassed: "I am afraid that this sort of thing is not as uncommon as it ought to be. The guards would be used to it. They would merely hide their rifles and pretend nothing was happening."

"I see. What sort of fellow is this Ras Matara?"

He shrugged elegantly: "A big, powerful man, an old-time chief. He is always heavily armed, and so are his men, about a couple of hundred soldiers. But . . ." He hesitated. "He is only fighting for what he thinks is his own hereditary right. He's never quite realized that this country has a central government—His Majesty the Emperor's. And as far as *we* are concerned . . . we are just intruders." He went on: "The story is that the prisoner was one of his distant cousins. But I think perhaps he was merely making himself known to us, letting you know that he is still there. I do not think he means real harm."

"Well, perhaps I'd better go and have a talk with him. You think I'll be able to find him?"

"It will not be necessary, sir. Perhaps if Superintendent Howard went up there . . ." He added apologetically: "It should not be anyone who is very senior."

Bob was considerably alarmed. He said nothing.

I said: "I'll go and see His Excellency. See what he has to say about it."

The Governor was in a bad temper that morning. One of his clerks, a Greek, had been found selling the administration's cigarette rations on the market up in Harar, and I'd caught him at an awkward time.

He said, fuming: "Damnation, use your discretion about it. That's what you're here for. On a job like this, you must learn to be a diplomat. Come and see me this evening about this confounded clerk of mine."

"Yes, sir."

As I turned to go, he said quickly: "Oh dear, I'm being rather rude, aren't I? It's just . . . terribly upsetting. I would have trusted Pastroudis with my life, and I learn I can't even trust him with a case of cigarettes. It's quite disgraceful." He smiled and said: "Armina especially asked me to invite you round for dinner again soon. Will you come?"

"Of course, any time."

"Splendid. But do please handle that business with Ras Matara yourself. It's much better, really, if I don't even know about it."

Back at police HQ, I said to Bob: "How'd you like to try your hand on this one?"

"Well . . . if you say so, sir."

I asked the Adjutant if Ras Matara would put Howard down a well too. I was assured that he probably would not.

"All right," I said to Bob, "go and see this fellow, give him my compliments, and tell him I want my Inspector back. Don't return without him, understand? And don't stand for any damn nonsense."

"Yes, sir. Er . . . what sort of line should I take with him? Should I be firm, or . . ."

I said: "Use your discretion about it. That's what you're here for. On a job like this you have to learn to be a diplomat."

As soon as he had left the office, I detailed an Ethiopian policeman to go along on the train, keeping out of sight, and keeping an eye on poor Bob. He was to report back to me if there was any trouble.

And, five days later, the policeman returned. He was alone. He made out his report, in longhand, in a mixture of English, French, and Italian, and it took me all night to read it. But it was quite illuminating.

Bob Howard, it seemed, had found Ras Matara in his village a few miles from the railway track. He had demanded the prompt release of Inspector Dengel. He had also lectured him sternly on the wickedness of carrying his rifles on the railway line, and had threatened to arrest him and all his troops. Ras Matara, fortunately for Howard, had been so impressed and delighted with his audacity that he had promptly offered him a job as an officer in his own private guerilla army, and when Howard refused, he had insisted on feasting him regally while the question was pursued.

And an Ethiopian feast is really not something for the very young. It consists mostly of raw beef—ten pounds or so is an adequate serving—washed down with unlimited *tej*. And *tej*, too, is not for any but the hardiest.

Very properly (not to give offense) Bob had tackled the raw meat with considerable valor, and considerable *tej* to lessen the pain. The immediate sickness had been cured with brandy (a consignment of Remy Martin from Djibouti to Addis Ababa had been looted from the train a while back), and then, the next day, the discussion and its accompanying feast had started over.

He wasn't exactly a prisoner, the policeman wrote, but Ras Matara liked the young man and insisted that he remain a guest for a while. He was feeding him, wining him, and putting him to bed at night with the eager young girls from the village. Poor Bob Howard was making desperate attempts to get sober at least once in a while; he wasn't succeeding.

I decided I'd better do something about it. I went to find Ras Matara myself. I took the old steam train up the line.

I was delighted to learn that one of the sideline benefits of my position was that I had my own personal carriage which could be shunted onto the train whenever it was required—a holdover from the old autocratic days of the Italians which I saw no need to inhibit. Privilege is, no doubt, highly immoral, but like most things immoral, it is also very satisfying.

And so, comfortably installed with two servants in a small, rococo sort of coach that had its own kitchen and veranda, with my own personal Adjutant and a personal brakeman, I set out for Baroda on the train that left, in theory, but not in practice, at six o'clock in the morning. We were three hours late getting away, but that was quite normal; they had sent a car for me when the train was ready to leave.

Rumbling slowly along the steep track that led into the luscious mountains, it was easy to forget that we were traveling through some of the darkest, remotest, and most savage country in the world. The old steam train I chose had an air of lethargy about it that was very pleasant; the new Diesel trains traveled faster, and were more efficient, but this was one of the old steam engines, a four-six-four, that would have delighted any railway buff. I much preferred the leisurely pace of the old steamers which panted and puffed and struggled against the mountains with proper respect for them.

Besides, life was easier on the steam train; it was less organized, and there were plenty of unscheduled stops when camels were lying asleep on the track (the Diesel could not stop quickly enough and went right through them), or when the engineer saw some wild boar and fancied some pork for supper, or when the engine driver felt everybody would like to get off the train and pass the time of day with a group of bushmen along the track.

We pulled in slowly and painfully, chugging and hissing, to the tiny station that was in the center of Ras Matara's territory.

Standing on the hot red sand in the shade of the tall green acacia trees, the noises of the bush at violent discord with the raucous sounds of the engine which hissed and steamed in the heat, I watched the people about me with fascination. It was the most motley collection a man could wish for.

There was a van-Dyke-bearded Ethiopian gentleman of great charm and dignity who was receiving obeisance from the peasants, talking to them quietly and expressively while they stood around him, admiring his neat white jodhpurs and smart silk jacket; his Galla servant was running on bare feet, dressed in ragged shirt and shorts, carrying a small metal teapot up to the engine where, I knew, he would borrow a long-handled shovel, and thrust the pot into the engine's furnace and then come running back a moment later with tea for the master.

There was a huge, near-naked crowd spilling untidily out of the third-class carriages, mostly through the windows, getting all tangled up with their long spears and their cudgels and their bows and arrows, their baggage slung in bundles round their necks, their white teeth shining and their voices boisterous and cheerful, exchanging insults with the local villagers who stood watching these strange city people. They were all barefoot, but some of them carried shoes to use when, in the course of time, they should reach the capital, and this was a weighty indication of their superiority.

Their occupation of the train, which now deposited its entire load so deep in unknown and dangerous country, even for them, was a common bond that held them all together in one big family; so that perfect strangers, who in Dire-Daua would not have known each other, were slapping each other on the back and laughing and joking together, or putting on a semblance of nonchalance to prove that they had been on the train before. One or two of them, who were carrying long muzzle-loading rifles of Turkish or Portugese origin, glanced nervously at my uniform and hastily disappeared into the turbulence of the crowd. It was well known that arms were not to be carried on the railway—or within twenty feet of it—but it was not so well known yet that the new police department had decided not to be too zealous about such matters of local custom.

Close by was an alert and wary little group of tribesmen from the distant interior, who had come, I learned, more than two hundred miles to see this weird steel monster they had heard about even in their remote village. They stood on the line itself, ahead of the stationary train, their chief at their head with his spear at the ready, poised like a cat about to pounce; a tall, gaunt old man with hair piled high above his wide, intelligent forehead, his sons standing behind him ready to repel any assault should the train move in their direction. You could almost see the old man's heart beating as he stared in armed and ready amazement at the monster, not frightened, but weighing the odds against him and prepared to die if necessary. For him and his sons, the train was a reality that had suddenly imposed itself on a consciousness that had never before accepted it. And, therefore, it was a danger. And he was daring it to make a move, just one move, toward him. His spear was ready.

Two girls were playing childish games in the powdery sand, their lithe slim figures unbelievably agile, moving with the incredible feline grace of beautiful leopards, their young womanly breasts belying their childish laughter. One of them was quite naked; the other wore a string round her waist with a little leather pouch attached to it at the side. The naked one was about fifteen years old, and her face was long and narrow, like the Phoenicians whose blood might have run in her veins; her eyes were quite solemn and sad when she stopped laughing and stared at me. The other girl was perhaps two years older, and her face was pleasantly round and chubby; when she got a little older she would undoubtedly run to fat, but now she was charming and delightful. Like her friend's, her skin was tight and taut and glowing. Even her feet were well formed, and neither of them had the spindly legs so common nearer the coast.

Standing solitary and savage, as guardedly at rest as a feeding leopard, a lone Danakil warrior—slim, loin-clothed, armed with a long bow bound with elephant hair, and a quiver full of arrows as well as a spear and a sling—was watching them. The whole of his face was quite covered with his hair, which hung down in front in tight curls, completely covering his features, and through which only his sharp black eyes shone wildly. The resemblance to a sheep dog was not as apparent as it might seem; there is nothing terrifying about a sheep dog.

An enormously overweight Somali woman stood beside him, wrapped in a length of bright red and yellow and purple cloth from India, a twelve-foot length of trade cotton wound tightly round her waist and then up over one shoulder; when she took off the green Kashmiri shawl that was keeping the dust out of her hair, I saw with a little pang of excitement that she was wearing a necklace made from the tiny pottery beads, delicately colored and highly polished, that the Portugese traders had brought to Africa more than five hundred years ago. These beads can still be found there if you get far enough into the interior, and I though for a moment of offering her a price for them, but then she hitched her bundle on to the huge cheek of her behind and waddled off, her four-year-old son following her, her flat feet padding noiselessly in the dust. Then she sat down on her haunches, bared her breast, and fed the boy, who stood on sturdy, wide-spaced legs, his fists on his hips, suckling ferociously at the mountainous rotundity. The two young Ethiopian girls—were they Danakil too, I wondered?—stopped their playing and stared at her, bewildered by her enormity. One of them put a slim hand to her own young breast, and then ran off laughing.

A small crowd of villagers stood round the engineman's cab,

where the driver—an Arab from the coast—was holding forth to them on the wonders of his train, talking with arm-waving vigor, pointing out this and that, wallowing in their adulation, and gradually drawing them closer and closer to the pipe of the exhaust. Then, when he was satisfied that they were all in just the right spot, he reached up and pulled the cord, sending a powerful jet of hissing steam right into the middle of them. As they yelped and leaped away, he threw back his head and roared with laughter.

There was so much of interest to stare at.

The crowd from the train was settling down, squatting beside the tracks, or wandering off to find herbs and spices to take home with them, or staring at the up-country tribesmen who were as strange to them as they were to me. I tried very hard to inject myself into these surroundings, to become part of these people; but when I tried to wonder where they all came from, I could only wonder, instead, what I myself was doing there.

I wandered over to the inevitable station café to find some beer, and to ask about Ras Matara.

It was a simple adobe building, one room for the office, the bar, and the café, over which a dilapidated Greek in a wrinkled suit presided, patiently watching his Galla boys serving coffee and *tej* and tea and beer to those of the passengers who had money. The whitewashed walls were peeled and dirty, and someone had left a rifle lying on the floor. A soldier had taken all the available chairs—four wooden frames covered with animal skins—and was lying full length on them, fast asleep. The only attempt at decoration was a canvas painting hung on the wall which depicted, cartoon-style, a battle between the Ethiopians and the Egyptians. It was a little pharaohesque in aspect, and the blood which poured out of the severed heads was turning brown with age.

A huge and bearded Ethiopian, his barrel chest covered with

six or seven bandoliers, two rifles slung across his back, was drinking *tej* out of a bottle. He paused as I came in, and I saw one beady, alert eye watching me, and then he went on with his drinking. He was physically immense, with a hard, cruel face, and not at all the kind of man you would pick a fight with. I was quite sure that this was Ras Matara himself; the arrogance of authority was very plain.

Leaning against the bar, I ordered a bottle of *tej*.

The big Ethiopian came across and spoke to me. In tolerable English, he said: "You English. Why you drink *tej*, not beer?" He sounded friendly enough.

I said cheerfully: "I like *tej*, a good drink. Will you have some with me?"

He insisted: "Why? Beer not good for you?"

It was one of the peculiarities of the local beer, which was made in Addis Ababa, that, although its flavor was excellent, it caused an alarming tightening of the genital muscles; it was something to do with the water, and the army doctors were full of learned reasons, but no cure. It was a most painful symptom. You could stand for hours against the nearest bush without the slightest relief. It was a condition that used to send the troops scurrying in anxiety to the nearest M.O., but only time could cure it. So, making a vulgar gesture, I said: "It does a man no good, here."

He nodded wisely. "Then you drink *tej* with me."

He clapped his hands and a soldier came running forward and slapped a Maria Theresa silver dollar—still the only good currency once you leave the towns—on the counter. The Greek pushed it back nervously, refusing it, and the chief picked it up and threw it to the soldier.

As we drank, I said: "You know you're not supposed to be on the railway line, armed?"

He shrugged: "Who will stop me?"

"You must be Ras Matara." I told him my name.

He nodded: "Yes, I am Ras Matara, what you call Chief Matara. You hear about me?"

"I hear about you."

He looked at me for a while, adding things up, and said at last: "You must be new policeman chief, no?"

"Yes, I am. I drink to your health."

He swallowed his *tej* and said: "I got one of your men here, stay with me, all the time drunk. Two of your men, other one is Amhara, he stay down well."

"Yes, so I believe."

He squinted at me out of one wrinkled eye. "You angry?"

"No."

"Good." He tipped the bottle and filled our glasses. "We have some more *tej*. But this is not good, like the *tej* I make. Royal *tej*, more better. You come to my place sometime, I give you more better *tej*."

"Good. I'll do that."

"Maybe you come now?"

"No, thank you very much. I just came to pick up my officers, and then I'm on my way up to Addis Ababa."

"Nothing in Addis Ababa we don't got in my village. Plenty food, plenty drink, plenty girls. You like girls?"

"Of course. Who doesn't?"

"Some people. Your little officer doesn't."

I burst out laughing. This was one sidelight on poor Bob Howard that was unexpected, to say the least.

We drank and talked for a while, talking mostly about food, and hunting, and rifles, and women. He was an interesting man, a strong man, who held his independence and his chieftainship in the old-fashioned way, by his strength and his skill with his weapons, and by the force of his own character. I do not doubt that he was cruel; but he was also brave. I would not have liked him as an enemy, but sitting here in a shabby bar a thousand miles from anywhere, he was an exciting companion.

The Greek produced some round balls of goats' cheese in a can of olive oil, and the Ras stuck his thick strong fingers in and fished them out, handing them to me as we ate and drank and talked, and at last I realized that the train, my reminder of reality, my link with civilization, was still standing in the station, refilled with water, ready to go and waiting only for me.

I said a little thickly, feeling heavy with oil and cheese and *tej:* "I have to go now. What about my men?"

He shrugged: "You want them back maybe?"

"Have them at the station for me when the train returns from Addis Ababa the day after tomorrow. Both of them, okay?"

"Sure, sure, for you, anything."

"Are they all right?"

"Your white officer, Englishman like you, is drunk, he sleep all the time, get too drunk to stand up. Other man, Dengel his name, he's okay."

"He's not been hurt?"

"Is a little bit hungry, maybe."

"I said: "Then do me a favor, will you? Take him out of that damn well and give him a good meal. A couple of girls too, maybe."

"Sure, sure . . . Don't you worry no more about them."

"And have both of them here for me on the way back."

"They be here. I feed them, give them drink . . ."

He walked with me to the door and took my hand in a strong, paralyzing grip. I could hear the bones crunching.

"Sometime," he said, "sometime I come down to Dire-Daua, to your place. Take you back to my place. We have good time together."

I said: "You're a bandit, for God's sake. If you show up in Dire-Daua, the Governor would have a fit."

He waved an enormous hand. "No worry about your Governor. Your Governor good fellow. Your Governor like girls too."

One picked up the strangest information in the most unlikely places.

* * *

On the way back, two days later, both Howard and Dengel were waiting for me, as Ras Matara had promised. Dengel was none the worse for his temporary discomforts, though Howard was fatter and older and looked as dissipated as a Rumanian roué.

But the incident settled a problem of administration. As soon as I arrived at my HQ, I sent a signal to our Superintendent in Addis Ababa:

COMMISSIONER TO SUPERINTENDENT:
THE PRACTICE OF CATCHING CRIMINALS ON THE RAILWAY
LINE WILL CEASE FORTHWITH.

And we had no more trouble on *that* piece of our territory.

5

I spent the first few weeks at my new post trying to discover, and remedy, the ills of the previous administration.

They were mostly intangible; it was the South Africans, more than anything else, that had so upset the Ethiopians. Their record had been a good one; there was no overt police brutality, and everyone to whom I spoke on the subject admitted that their behavior had been courteous, their police work efficient, and their presence relatively unobtrusive.

Nonetheless, the spirit of apartheid was too deeply ingrained in them to permit the realization of the Amhara's enormous pride, self-reliance, and dignity. And this spirit showed itself in tiny, unwitting insults that were usually never really intended.

What is left of the class system in the Western countries is still founded, today, on some sort of quality, positive or negative—on money, heritage, manners and customs, or social circumstance. Apartheid, as practiced in South Africa, insists that the main division is an ethnic one, that the black man is *ipso facto* a lesser being.

Maybe among the tribes in the far south they've got away with it successfully; the Zulu *impis* have not struggled very hard against their oppressors since Chief Dinizulu, son of the famous Cetywayo, surrendered to the British in 1888 and was exiled to St. Helena for his pains. But among the Amhara, the idea behind apartheid is an intolerable affront.

The history of Africa, by and large, is the history of colonialism, which in turn meant, at the peak of its acceptance all over the world, the exploitation of one race by another. And at one time, we must remember, this was not thought to be morally reprehensible; the *mores* change just as fast, just as inexorably, as the *tempora*. Less than a century ago, the British colonial endeavors in Africa, in India, in Southeast Asia, and over half the face of the globe were considered to be as just and as permissible as the American conquests in Cuba, Guam, or the Philippines, or those of France, Spain, or Portugal elsewhere. There was no national philosophy involved; it was a question of different times.

But in the slicing up of Africa, one country—and only one—stood defiant, and successfully so. Ethiopia was never part of any colonial empire except for the five years following the 1936 assault by the armies of Mussolini—and even that was merely an occupation of vital areas rather than a total conquest.

Long accustomed to invasion attempts by the Persians, the Arabs, the Egyptians (and on occasion the British too), Ethiopia had always held out and maintained its fiery independence. When the white man took over all the countries over her borders, Ethiopia stood on her own two feet and held on to her integrity through a combination of the impregnability of her terrain and the enormous strength of her fighting qualities.

Her resistance to the overpowering logistic might of the Italian armies of Graziano had been phenomenal; she had suffered the most terrible attrition; and now, after five long years of subjugation, she was suffering the indignity of a benevolent occupation by her allies and was being told to step off the pavement for the white man.

I never cease to wonder that Ethiopia didn't take matters into her own hands and solve that problem in her own way too; it is greatly to her credit that she showed such restraint.

There was, for example, the matter of the hospital.

Like any other, Dire-Daua's hospital consisted of private rooms and public wards—the old class-system at work, the privacy of a room for those who could afford it, or a bed in a dormitory for those who could not.

In the police force under the South Africans, the private rooms were reserved for the whites, the dormitories for the blacks. The lowest white rank had his privacy, the highest black rank shared with twenty or thirty others. I switched this to a class division that the Ethiopians could appreciate (and was also in keeping with my own understandings as a long-time army officer)—the private rooms for officers, the wards for the other ranks, regardless of the arbitrary distinction of color.

I found that the senior positions were open only to whites; I changed that too. I found a similar distinction in the rationing—the Ethiopians were being fed, officially, with the *posho,* the ground wheat supplied to African troops in Kenya, which the Ethiopian—a natural gourmet—won't eat. I changed that too.

It was in the little things . . .

But I soon found that the imposition of my own form of snobbery—which I will always defend—fitted very nicely into the feudal pattern of our host country. They, too, are snobs; it just happens that their form of snobbery is not based on pigmentation. Trash is trash, they would say, whether it's white or black, and a man's quality has little to do with his color as such. (They will state, nonetheless, that too black a skin is often a sign of Bantu blood, which they consider inferior). But in the aggregate, their philosophy is widely opposed to apartheid.

I found that the old colonial barriers disappeared with remarkable speed and ease, and we all settled down to an easygoing existence in which those intangible little indignities were no longer a problem.

And I found, to my great pleasure, that we were all very popular all of a sudden.

*   *   *

I discussed the color question, briefly, with the Duke of Harar when we finally met, officially, at a reception at the Governor's house. Even here, there was a touch of comic opera.

Sir Reginald said, whispering to me and smiling quietly: "He's not supposed to be here, really, because unofficially he represents the Ethiopian Government itself, by virtue of his position. The Emperor's youngest son, official or not, it's bound to indicate a certain . . . acceptance. I shouldn't really have invited him, but dammit, he practically invited himself. And he's such a nice young man."

I met his current mistress here too, the half-Italian girl I'd seen him with on the first night of my arrival. Her name was Maria Teslata, a tall, leggy, blond-haired, coffee-colored young woman with a very vivacious air about her, more Italian to look at, more Amhara in her manner. She was constantly by his side, and they had a tendency to hold hands all the time.

We sat on the veranda together, on the slightly-smelling

hide chairs, and he sipped his drink and said: "So apartheid's been thrown out, is that why they sent you here?"

I said: "Yes, I believe that's part of it."

"I'm glad. But tell me something . . ." He was probing, gently needling. "Are you subjugating your own instincts to the demands of your office? If you are, it's highly immoral, wouldn't you say?"

"Would you rather I subjugated my office to the demands of my instinct?"

"It's a moot point, isn't it?"

"Not really. I'm a monarchist by nature."

"But a black king is still a black man."

The Emperor Haile Selassie is probably the only statesman left in the world; they've all become politicians nowadays. I said: "There's not a man in Europe who doesn't regard your father with both admiration and affection."

"Ah, but he's not black. He's brown." He said slyly: "I'm the only really black one in the family. They all frown on it. It's not supposed to be a good color here, the color of the *jambos.*"

"The *jambos?*"

He gestured vaguely. "The East Africans. Kenya, Tanganyika, Uganda. Where all our slaves come from. It's a bad color, black, not a single really black man at the Court. When I become Emperor, I'll have to change all that, won't I?"

His brother, the Duke of Gondar, the eldest son, was heir to the throne.

I said: "If you have to wait for Gondar to die, that might be a very long time. He's still a young man."

He nodded. "And dull. The right color, but dull." He looked at me and said: "Did you know that Gondar's going to be assassinated when my father dies?"

I couldn't help staring at him, but he didn't seem very upset about it. I said nothing, and he went on: "Nothing to do with me, of course, I rather like him, but . . . there are forces at work that neither I nor my father can control. They think I'd make a better ruler, and they're probably right, so . . ." He shrugged. "I'm not giving away any state secrets, it's fairly well known. I know it, my father knows it, Gondar himself knows it."

"And he accepts it?"

"He accepts it."

"You too?"

He nodded. "Yes, me too. I'll be working with the right people, even if their ideas are not always correct. I hope to be able to change them."

"And why are you telling me this?"

He laughed. "Just planting seeds, something to talk about." Slipping easily from one thought to another, he said: "I saw you were chatting with Maria. A fascinating young woman, isn't she?"

"She's gorgeous."

"They all want me to get married, to some peasant child from the interior, strengthen the bonds, all that damn nonsense. I'm fighting it, but I won't be able to hold out much longer."

I said, wondering about it: "And what will happen to Maria after your wedding?"

It was very easy to talk with him on personal matters.

"Oh . . ." He shrugged. "I'll send her away for a short time, just to satisfy the conservatives in the government. A week or two, perhaps. After that, she can come back again. As a Copt, of course, I'm only allowed one wife, I sometimes wish I were a Moslem and could have a few more, make things a lot easier, wouldn't it?"

I said: "Well, there's precedent, isn't there? Menelik's grandson, what was his name?"

"Ah yes, Lij Yasu became a Moslem, but he spent fifteen years in chains until he died, as a result of it. That's not for me . . ." His mind was jumping about again. He said: "What do you think of our host?"

I said: "That's a hell of a question. I like him. I like him very much."

"Yes, he's a good man." He waved his hands vaguely. "You'd never have got away with all these changes if he weren't. What about the Magallo barricade?"

I wondered what he was driving at. I said: "As far as I can gather, it's as much to keep us away from there, as it is to keep them away from us. No one seems to be stopped if they're coming this way."

"It's not very nice to have a barbed-wire barricade through the middle of a town."

"So let's get rid of it."

He was suddenly laughing again. He said: "You'll have to tell Reggie it was your idea, not mine. A question of protocol."

"Yes, of course. Why can't I go over to the Magallo without having my throat cut?"

He stared at me. "Who on earth told you that?"

"Everybody tells me that."

"Well, it's nonsense. Absolute nonsense. What do you think we are, a pack of black savages?" Not changing the subject, he said: "I hear you're off to Jig-Jigga tomorrow."

"Yes, I am."

"Well, then, don't you realize that the road to Jig-Jigga goes through our territory all the way to the Madar Pass, you can't even get to Jig-Jigga without passing through our territory. Harar too, you've got to drive right through the town to get there. *Ours.* And that reminds me, there's a convoy of trucks coming in from Mogadiscio tomorrow, heading for Harar, a big load of spare parts for Diesel trucks. Do me a favor and let it through your customs, will you?"

"Yes, of course, if you wish. What's it carrying besides spare parts?"

"Oh, nothing else. The only other thing I smuggle is perfume, and that comes from Djibouti, on the train. Talk to Reggie, he'll tell you all about it." He clapped his hands for the Somali servant, and when his glass had been refilled he got up and said: "One of your young officers is making a pass at Maria, I'd better go and rescue her, poor thing. She never knows when someone's trying to get her into a bed."

I saw that she was talking with Inspector Clifton, a small, eager, very young man who had just arrived from England. He was thin and slight and excitable, and he was nodding his head vigorously at her and staring at the V between her breasts. I made a mental note to have a word with him in the morning, about protocol.

I found the Governor standing alone and looking forlorn, worrying about whether the staff were looking after things properly, and he said nervously: "Is it going all right, do you think? I hate these things, I really hate them . . ."

I said: "Where's Armina tonight?"

He grimaced: "I sent her out shopping for the evening. Doesn't really do any good, but . . ."

I told him about Harar's cryptic remarks, and he said, whispering: "Oh yes, he smuggles things, all the time. His allowance from the Emperor apparently is not very high, and so he's got this trucking company, some old Italian trucks he seized, he brings in machinery, wines, all sorts of things. Technically, it's smuggling, but into their territory, and so, when it passes through ours, it's nice if we can look the other way."

"Doesn't the Ethiopian government try to stop it?"

"Yes, once in a while. His father sends a senior customs man down sometimes, but the Duke simply puts him in jail for a while, no trouble. After all, Harar is his personal Duchy, so it's really none of our business, is it? You're sure everything's going well?"

I said, meaning it: "It couldn't be better."

*   *   *

At midnight, when Harar and Maria had gone (we had to push-start his Lancia to get it going), I excused myself for a breath of air and wandered down into the silent riverbed, over the soft sand to the barricade, and told the sentry there to open it up and leave it open, permanently.

I crossed over to the jumble of adobe and stone houses, lit with the yellow, smoky flare of kerosene lamps, and found a café, a single, frontless room with half a dozen rickety tables inside and at the opening. A small boy, not more than seven or eight years old, was solemnly watering the dirt floor from an old gasoline can, to keep the dust down.

A few Ethiopians, five or six of them, were sitting there drinking beer and tej, and they rose courteously at my greeting — *"te'ena ysterling, God be with you"*—and I sat on the edge of the storefront and ordered beer. A young man came and sat at my table and stared at me for a while, and then the owner chased him away by cuffing his ears, and then two or three young men came and sat on the sand just outside and stared at me, saying nothing.

I watched the donkeys go by, and the women bowed low under huge piles of wood on their backs, and the tiny children shepherding the goats and chasing the chickens. And then, the young men sitting in the sand were joined by a few more, and a few more, and soon there were twelve or thirteen of them, just squatting and staring, saying nothing, neither friendly nor hostile, but just interested.

I had another bottle of beer, and then another, and at last,

59

when I got up to go home, there were more than thirty Magallans, mostly very young, mostly men, sitting around outside the café. Someone had brought a Coleman pressure lamp and had set it on a wooden stool nearby. I stepped carefully over them all, and one of them got up, laughing, and pointed, and said in broken Italian: *"E li, la ragazza, the girl is over there."*

He was pointing to a small, shuttered house across the dirt road, a single room with a roof of old, straightened-out cans. A young girl was standing in the doorway, beckoning me; one of the local brothels. The young man laughed again and said: *"Beh, andiamo insieme."*

I thought I might be pushing my luck a little too hard, so I shook my head and said: *"Abbiamo anche noi, we have them too."*

As I walked down to the riverbed, the little crowd came with me, still saying nothing, still just being there. They stopped at the edge where the soft sand started, like an escort to see me home, and I went to the barricade and saw that it had been fastened open with a couple of iron-wood stakes. It was never closed again.

The Governor's house was dark, the guests all gone home, but Armina was there, leaning over the veranda in the darkness.

I said: "You missed a good party, Armina. How are you?"

We stood there under the bougainvillea in the silence, the night cool and friendly now, and chatted quietly for a while.

She said: *"Dove sei state, where were you?"*

"In the Magallo."

"The Magallo? They'll kill you over there."

"No, I think not."

"Ethiopians." I felt that she wanted to spit. "Why you don't go to Somali quarter? Is better."

"Tomorrow, I'm off to Jig-Jigga, all the Somalis in the world there."

"Jig-Jigga? You bring me back a Somali shawl?"

"All right."

"A green one. But a good one, from Kashmir, you know?"

"All right. Is Reggie asleep?"

"In bed, he doesn't sleep till I come to him."

"Tell him it was a very good party."

"I tell him. You won't forget my shawl?"

"I won't forget. Good-night, Armina."

"Buona notte."

I walked around the deserted streets for a while, went home, and went to bed.

Tomorrow, Jig-Jigga; the long steep drive up the mountain to Harar, the winding road through the silence of the Madar Pass, and the great gray plain of the disputed Ogaden.

6

The road from Dire-Daua, up the escarpment and down the other side to the rich bright valley where all the game was, was a fascinating place. Someone had once called it the Valley of Despair, and at first sight this seemed a good name for it.

It was an awesome and eerie place. Down between the steep red mountains, the grass was green and the trees were tall, but there was an uncanny silence, an almost frightening absence of any of the more common and friendly noises. There was no human habitation, and the scurrying, ratlike hyrax seemed to set the mood as they peered nervously from their tiny hideouts on the red rock-shelf, and then darted back in alarm into the purple shadows to crouch there, rodent noses twitching, tiny ears sharply alerted, whiskers bristling with fear.

Sometimes a leopard coughed, and sometimes there was the

distant moan of a lion's muted roar; on occasion, the roar was closer, and then one heard the deep base notes as well, not just the higher-pitched beginnings of it that traveled farther and sounded like a wail. But always there was the feeling that, for some indefinable reason, it would not be safe to leave the comforting security of the truck, or at least, not to get too far away from the well-defined red rut of the track.

It was a strange feeling, because a man is safer in the deepest, remotest bush than he is on the streets of any major city; but an atavistic and quite senseless fear was part of the aura of the Madar Pass. The pass is majestic, awesome, and strikingly beautiful, richly sprouted with bright green plants in the red sand; but there is a strange and unaccountable menace that seems to hang over it. I never once moved through the pass without experiencing this sense of malediction.

In the sand, even the noise of the tires was silenced, and there was always an overwhelming urge to sound the horn; and having done so, one felt that the great red rocks that towered high in the air, perched on their slender pinnacles, would come tumbling down like some biblical avenger.

These rocks were an astonishing sight. Over the years, the soil had been washed away by the torrential rains of the winter, and in receding had left great boulders as big as houses perched delicately on top of tall, pointed spikes of harder sandstone, two or three hundred feet high, that looked as though a sneeze would bring them crashing down. Some of these monstrous rocks, fifty, sixty, even a hundred feet across, were balanced ridiculously on pointed skeletal tapers no more than a few inches round at the top, so that they seemed to hang high above your head ready to fall down at the drop of a hat. Sometimes they did fall; there was no warning, no tremulous quiver, but suddenly a pinnacle would unexpectedly crumble and its huge burden would drop ponderously down in a flurry of red dust, seeming to settle almost gently on the earth after so many centuries of lordly elevation in the skies.

But the valley was one of those places that need to be understood, like a beautiful African girl whose apparent savagery hides a compelling warmth. It spread out on both sides of the track, here broad, there narrowly confined between high sandstone bluffs where the rock badgers hid. Yellow-necked partridge wandered about in profusion, and slowly, idiotic guinea fowl twisted their slim necks in disdain, and sometimes a great bustard would go galloping across the sand in a slow and laborious takeoff, its primeval wings flapping fantastically like something out of Charles Adams' imagination.

Always there were gazelle, and kudu, and oryx, and at night, when the alarm and the loneliness were more apparent, the bright sharp eyes of hyena would catch the truck's headlights; not just a few of them, as one usually saw in the daytime, but unbelievable hundreds, even thousands, great swaying waves of tiny bright lights that danced like mayflies.

And then, their paws could be heard beating into the sand; not softly, as foxes do, but with a heavy sound like galloping horses, thundering past and wheeling back into the bush again.

Everywhere the tall thorn trees thrust their gnarled trunks high up to the broad bright umbrellas of their flat green tops, and thick vines with yellow fleshy pods, looking somehow poisonous (they were) were everywhere intertwined with coarse gray shrub and wait-a-bit thorns that tore viciously at your clothing.

It had an endless fascination. And above all, it was silent.

It was almost a relief, a relief from a somehow masochistic pleasure, to see the sudden gap in the hills which meant the end of the Valley of Despair and the entry into the great dry plain of the Ogaden.

Here, the undefined boundary was at its clearest—the change from the highlands of Ethiopia proper to the barren desert of the Somali tribes. And as you left the green grass and the rocks, unexpectedly, you found a coffee shop.

It was a far cry from the coffee shops of the western world. It was merely a small enclosure of thorn branches pulled into a careless circle, a defensive perimeter called a *zeriba*, in which was a wood fire, a single chair carved out of a solid trunk of thorn tree, and a piece of matting thrown over some rickety sticks to provide a piece of shade. A little to one side stood the one-room mud house of the owner, whose name was Gusala.

Gusala was an Ethiopian, a tall, well-built man with small black eyes that were always ready to wrinkle up in the delight that only a simple man can ever enjoy. He was slim at the hips and deep chested, and in his ragged clothes of discarded army khaki he would have given the impression that he was worthy of better circumstances, except for one thing—he was perfectly happy just as he was.

In this coffee shop you were expected to bring your own drinking vessel, and Gusala would make a thick black brew from wild coffee beans, standing discreetly in the background while you waited, and his wife, a cheerful, buxom woman of thirty or so whose name was Shwaya, would stand at the door of the house with her innumerable children gathered round her, all silently watching, while the water boiled over the twig fire and the scent of wood smoke hung in the hot air. If you did not have your own mug, then Gusala was ready; there was one glass, which was a treasured possession and kept wrapped up in a piece of rag. True, it was only an old beer bottle cut down to make a drinking vessel, but even old beer bottles were hard to come by here. (I once gave Gusala half a dozen empty bottles, and watched him cut them into glasses. Three parts full of water, a thin film of oil floating on the top—oil from a passing truck—and a red-hot spearhead thrust suddenly into it . . . and presto, the top shears neatly off.)

With the hot sun beating down, and the dust flying across

the plain in front of you, with the warm mystery of the valley close behind you, you would sit on the solitary stool and look at the magnificent view and realize that this, really, was all a man could ever desire.

Gusala's house was tiny. It was filled to overflowing with children and chickens and goats, and Gusala always slept outside, by the fire.

One night, shortly after my arrival, there was a happy, astonished commotion in the village of Jig-Jigga that lay only a mile or so below his compound, and the word *libah . . . libah* was on every Somali's lips. *Libah* means lion, and Gusala had killed one that night, almost with his bare hands, and I heard the story from an admiring crowd:

Gusala was sleeping by his fire, pleasantly full of raw venison and *tej*, when he suddenly awoke in the still blackness to feel a hot breath on his face. Attracted by the smell of a kudu's carcass, which Gusala had left hung up in the branches of the thorn tree to keep it out of reach of hyena, a lion had crept through the flimsy thorn fence and silently dragged it down. There was a great deal of meat left (which was fortunate) and the lion had satisfied his hunger silently, while Gusala slept on unwakened by the slow persistent crunching of the dead animal's bones. At last, replete, the lion had wandered about the compound sniffing curiously, as lions will, at everything in sight.

One of these things was Gusala.

Gusala felt the hot breath on his face. He suddenly awoke, looked up to see the great yellow head close to his, swung round on his side, and delivered a resounding blow with his fist on the lion's nose. I never found out just why he did this. When I asked him, he said modestly that it was the proper thing to do, but I rather suspect that it was a desperate, instinctive reaction, though most of us, I feel, would have reacted by dying of fright; a lion is an enormous animal at such close quarters.

In any event, Gusala struck the lion on the snout, leaped to his feet and seized a burning log from the fire, and so belabored the poor animal's head with it that it turned and tried to force its way through the thorn *zeriba* again. Seeing it turn, Gusala dropped his log, drew his dagger, and threw himself on the lion's back, stabbing again and again and again till finally it dropped dead at his feet.

And what's more, he had the carcass to prove it.

Thereafter, Gusala's coffee shop assumed a heightened prestige, and ever afterward, whenever I stopped there to pass the time of day, there were two or three of the villagers squatting about the compound chatting with him, listening attentively to what he had to say.

In the village itself, his name became famous overnight, and little groups of people would wander up the steep road to the head of the pass merely to visit him and say they had spoken with the great Gusala, the man who had killed a lion with his bare hands. (At the fourth or fifth telling, the dagger came to be left out, and the later versions were that Gusala had strangled the lion.) He delighted in the sudden access of fame, and would show his visitors the great tawny skin that hung over the door of his hut. The fame never went to his head; he remained a modest, wise, and lovable man, still content to sit by his fire and watch the splendid panorama of the plain below him, maintaining the dignity of his household by keeping his young wife permanently pregnant, and bringing his children up to fear no man, nor beast, nor devil.

I regret to say that sometime later a Somali sneaked in one night and stole Gusala's lion skin, an indignity from which he never really recovered. Had it been another Ethiopian, Gusala would have searched him out and killed him, but a despised Somali . . . It just wasn't worth the trouble.

Thereafter, his café was off limits to Somalis.

*   *   *

The significance of Gusala's achievement can only be appreciated if one understands the absolute terror in which these lions sometimes held the town. There are a great many tales to support the view that the lion is quite harmless unless he is hungry, and indeed, this is probably true.

But there's the rub. When game is short for one reason or another, he often *is* hungry, and how can you tell? A flat belly is an indication, but if you're close enough to study the belly you are too damn close if it happens to be time for a meal. And there's always the urgent question of the lion turned man-eater.

A man-eater, generally speaking, is a lion who has grown too old or decrepit to catch his natural food and therefore turns to slower game—man. But not always so; a young lion can catch the habit and come to regard *Homo sapiens* as a tasty change from zebra or gazelle, in just the same way as man acquires a taste for oysters or rattlesnake steaks. His cunning, his stealth, and above all, his enormous strength (usually grossly underestimated) make him a very formidable adversary.

If there are man-eaters in the area, there's only one possible answer: get out your gun.

Here, in Jig-Jigga, the townspeople had long been plagued by a small pride of lions that were beginning to be a considerable danger. And when at last I reached the police building in the bright cool of the early morning, I found a crowd of twenty or thirty Somalis hanging around the courtyard. Some of them carried a sack, a hammocklike arrangement of burlap which they slung between them. I heard the word *libah* and said to the Adjutant:

"Looks as though they've killed one of those man-eaters at last. Let's have a look at it."

Not stopping to think, I signaled the Somalis to drop their burden on the paved floor of the yard, and said: "Open it up."

68

They dropped their bundle. One of them gathered his loincloth about him, passed his stick and his sling and his spear across to one of the others, and knelt down beside it. When he unwrapped it, I felt my stomach turning.

It was half a man. . . . There was the chest, the arms, and the head; no more. The body, from the stomach downward, was gone. In the sallow, bloodless head, there were two deep holes, one on each side of the skull, where the lion's great teeth had gently inflicted the silent, mortal wound. The white ribs showed in the red, unholy cavity, which was hollow, and empty, and somehow terribly mocking.

I turned away sharply and went into the building.

* * *

I spent the morning over the dull administrative matters that were waiting for me—one murder, four cases of theft, two cases of camel killing, and the release from the local prison of all the minor offenders who were using the jail as a hotel.

This was always a problem in those parts. The bush offers a certain adequate way of life under normal circumstances, but the towns, such as Jig-Jigga, were always a magnet for the young bloods of the outlying tribes. Being desert Somali, they lived entirely on camel's milk, with nothing else to supplement their diet, and when they came to town for the first time and found they had left the protective security of their own tribe, they found themselves, frequently, to be hangers-on in a society that really didn't care very much about them. The urban pleasures, as opposed to their own bucolic existence, were always enticing, and so they would continue to hang on, and slowly starve.

It was not a question of shortage of work; work is anathema to a desert Somali, perhaps very properly so. With his own tribe, he would herd the camels and milk them, and from his earliest days he was taught that work was only for the Mitgan tribe, the untouchables of the Somalilands.

But in the towns the young men would soon find out that it was not necessary either to work or to starve; they could break a minor law and be put in jail for ten days, where they sat around doing nothing all the time and were fed three times a day. Upon release, they would promptly steal some trivial object, bring it to the police station, and turn themselves in once more. (The common name for jail throughout most of East Africa is "King George's Hotel.")

Our solitary murderer was quite happy. He had killed his brother, and the rest of the family were after his blood, so jail was the safest place for him. During the previous administration he had been tried and convicted and sentenced to hang (under the Ethiopian Penal Code), but we had no hangman or gallows, and since I personally have always been opposed to capital punishment, we sort of let it all drag on, hoping that something would turn up. By Ethiopian custom, blood money can be paid in lieu of punishment, and this, in time, did happen.

The women's quarters in the jail had a minor problem: a Somali woman had fought with an Ethiopian woman and torn her dress to shreds, and I was expected to do something about it. The clothes the women wore were prison clothes, Mother-Hubbard-type dresses stitched up on the prison sewing machine for them because their own clothes, if they wore any (in the bush, some went naked, some wore a string, some wore a kind of a skirt), were usually infested with lice and had to be baked in the prison oven.

On this occasion, I had the two young women brought before me with great solemnity, lectured them both on the evils of fighting, and then took a leaf out of Solomon's Book and took the Somali girl's dress away from her and gave it to the Ethiopian, thereby satisfying everybody concerned. There was no shame for the Somali girl in her nakedness; it was simply that when they were released they usually kept the homemade dresses and would tear them up for very useful bags and continue to go naked.

I told the men of the Duke of Harar's convoy that was on its way up from Mogadiscio with smuggled spares for his trucks, told them not to disturb it, and was glad to see that they all nodded wisely and agreed that this was very correct, and by twelve o'clock my day was finished. I went with the senior Ethiopian officer, Inspector Tafeta, to look at the town.

I said: "We'll have to do something about those lions, what do you think?"

He nodded. "Yes, I think so. They took two children last week."

"A big pride?"

"Five of them, three fully grown, two young ones. They came into the town, right into the marketplace last night. I don't like that."

"Well, what are the local people doing about it?"

He shrugged. "The Somalis are hunting them, but so far without any success at all. Perhaps if we organized a hunt, a big one . . . We should invite the Governor down, he's a good man on a lion hunt, he knows as much about lions as an Ethiopian." He grinned and said: "Or a Somali."

"All right, I'll arrange it."

An incongruous sort of place, Jig-Jigga, just a mass of adobe, one- or two-room huts in the middle of an immense desert, but housing two hundred thousand people, the only water for miles around, and consequently a marketplace of some importance.

He was a big man, Tafeta, plump and hearty, with a sly, quiet manner that was most disarming.

He said: "Why don't we go and watch them throwing the water? A very big herd came in today."

In the whole of the Ogaden, roughly the size of Arizona,

71

there is only one so-called river, the Nogal. And it's permanently dry except when the *tug*, the deadly wall of water twenty feet high, comes racing down it once or twice a year when the rains in the distant mountains flood the hills. But here, the wells are deep and good, and permanently full of sweet water, untainted by the gypsum sand which is all the Ogaden consists of. And, as Tafeta had said, a herd had come in for its bi-weekly watering.

We walked over to watch.

One of the best wells lies on the outskirts of the town, and is about sixty feet deep, with a diameter of about six feet. There is no concrete wall in the accepted pattern, but a succession of logs instead, logs cut from the *guda* thorn trees that flourish in the mountains of Ethiopia proper, brought here on the backs of groaning camels many, many years ago. They are laid one across the other in log-cabin form, leaving a space for the water to seep through; no one knows when the well was built, nor how long these same logs have been there, and no one ever does any maintenance on them. But they serve the purpose. Using these horizontal timbers as steps, a man can climb down into the well easily enough. At the bottom, there is usually about four or five feet of water.

Outside the well, lying foundationless on the hard sand, there is a long watering trough, quite shallow, and very crudely made. The cement has been bleached bone white by the sun, and here and there it has been patched with adobe.

The normal procedure for filling the trough is quite simple. You simply lower a water bag on a sixty-foot length of rope, and haul it up. The bag is a goatskin which has been tightly stitched and bees-waxed at the belly and the legs (where the animal was cut open for skinning), with an opening at the neck to serve as a spigot. When it is full, it looks rather depressingly like a bloated, purple, headless animal with its limbs sticking out obscenely into the air; it glistens moistly. And the porous

72

nature of the leather itself causes it to leak slightly, so that a gentle and continuous evaporation keeps the water cool. After a few generations of use, the skin loses its original rancid taste, and a good waterskin, which leaks just the right amount, is considered a very prized possession.

The rope will be made of camel's hair into which goat's hair has been twisted for added strength. Or sometimes it will be made of tightly woven raffia, when it looks like an enormously long pigtail cut from a blonde giantess.

But when the herd to be watered is a large one, then the conventional filling of the trough by this method is too slow, and the camels, ill-tempered and obstreperous at the best of times, become quite unmanageable. And this is where the "throwing" of the water comes in.

On such occasions in a market town of this size, there are often spectators, for the sight is a fascinating one even to the Somalis themselves; it is part of their normal way of life, but nonetheless the expertise is a question of tribal honor, and therefore it attracts a great deal of attention. Besides, there is always the chance that someone will fall and break his fool neck, and this is a good thing for rival tribesmen to witness.

As soon as the herd is sighted, just a nebulous cloud of dust on the far horizon, the watchers begin to gather around the wells. They tuck their skirts delicately between their thighs and squat on the sand, bony knees upthrust, or stand still on one leg (they will stand like this for hours) bracing one foot against a knee and leaning on their spears in their characteristic position, and they will watch the throwing and argue about it incessantly, for the Somali is a great talker. It is here and now that the tribal intrigues are hatched, for there is nothing the Somali likes better than scheming someone else's downfall. There will be a lot of argument about who is going to do the actual throwing of the water, because work is regarded as an undignified proceeding which should be done only by animals, women, and white men, in that order of importance. And undoubtedly there will be a lot of discussion about the Somali's only other love—the camel.

But at last, with the bad-tempered and thirsty beasts milling around impatiently, the work will begin.

A dozen men will clamber down into the well and brace themselves firmly against the timbers, one above the other, so that each man's head is close by the feet of the man above him. The lowest man stands in the water, up to his waist or throat, and the highest man straddles the top with his feet widespread, and between them there is a living ladder of lithe and supple bodies, glistening with sweat, their loincloths tucked tightly round their slim waists. Each man carries a hollow gourd, its capacity perhaps a gallon or so. The chief camel herder will call for water, and the throwing will begin.

The bottom man scoops up a gourdful of water, and throws it to the man above him. This man, in turn, drops his empty gourd down and catches the full one; he throws the full one up to the man above him, and catches the empty one which this man, in turn, drops to him, then drops it to the bottom man, who scoops up the water, throws it up, and catches the next empty one. In ten or twelve such movements, the first full gourd comes to the top, is emptied into the trough, quickly returned, then dropped stage by stage to the bottom again.

Now, almost certainly, the chain breaks.

Perhaps it is a remark someone has made down below that has started an argument. Perhaps someone has missed his footing on the wet timbers. Or perhaps the timing went wrong somewhere.

So the whole thing grinds to a halt and there are angry words all round, with the camels, excited now, beginning to fight each other and their herders. And then, it starts again.

This time, everyone checks his position to make sure he is firmly braced and that his arms and shoulders have free play

74

for the fast movement required of them. And this time, some-one calls out a sort of "one . . . two . . . three." Only it is usually: "Aiyah . . . aiyah . . . aiyah." And the long ladder comes to sudden life again.

One gourd up and one gourd down, with the top man throwing the water into the trough and sending the empty yellow container back underarm with the reverse swing of the same motion, and catching the next full one as it comes in. The speed gets faster and faster, gently increasing until the peak is reached, and to the spectator it is bewildering. Each upward movement (full) brings down another gourd (empty) on its backstroke, and the rhythmic precision is astonishing.

The water pours into the trough in tight little gushes, and for an hour now the motion will not be arrested; it's as constant and mechanical as a village pump. One up, one down . . . one up, one down . . . The chain does not break. The movement does not falter.

Standing there in the broiling sun with Tafeta, I checked my watch. At the height of the rythm, the *smack, smack, smack* of delicate hands on the thin-shelled, shining yellow gourds kept precise time with the second hand. I timed it again, and in the space of two minutes, a hundred and twelve gourds of water were emptied into the trough. That's over three thousand gallons an hour, which is pretty incredible for unaided muscle power from sixty feet underground.

It seems hardly believable. To the tick of an average watch, with a cadence as infallible as a metronome, the pumping went on for more than an hour, nonstop, monotonous, and almost hypnotic.

*   *   *

75

It raises a question frequently asked. The belief is fairly common that the African is stronger physically than the white man, and certainly few white men could keep up the untiring rhythm of water throwing for very long. But this is not always true, though the men of some tribes are indeed gifted with phenomenal strength.

Not so the Somali. He is thin, lithe, delicate, and astonishingly brittle. In these parts, his diet is almost entirely limited to camel's milk. Indeed, among the true desert tribes a little to the south, milk is the *only* article of diet. The camels are milked, and the produce shared out among, first, the men, then the children, and then the women. If there is not enough to go round, it's the women who suffer, but this is of little consequence to them; the society here is strictly patriarchal.

In the towns, where there is a relative sophistication, this diet is supplemented with vegetables, which are expensive, and an occasional piece of meat, which is very cheap indeed. In spite of the abundance of game, on which the Ethiopians live, the Somali believes that hunting is work, and therefore taboo. Indeed, only the Mitgan, the untouchables, will hunt; and it is for precisely this reason that they are regarded with such contempt. In terms of Western understanding, the average Somali's diet is disastrously inadequate. Camel's milk is rich and thick and very tasty, but it is not enough by itself to support a proper existence. So that although their endurance is very impressive, their actual strength is not. Though they will cover sixty miles a day through the desert on foot and keep it up for days on end, they have the muscles of very young children. They exist because they have learned how to keep going.

I once met a camel herder who was walking from Garoe to Galkayu, a distance of a hundred and eighty miles, carrying no more sustenance than a leaky goatskin that held less than a half-gallon of sour water. It was empty when I found him, and he still had more than half the journey to go. He drank, in my presence, there and then, the entire contents of a four-gallon water can, his empty belly swelling alarmingly in the process until he looked like a pregnant woman. So fortified, he continued his march, scorning to ride in my truck because it was a device of the heathen, and as such beneath his dignity. He was at pains to explain most carefully that the water was a different matter; without it he would have died, but God had sent me to him in time. He didn't really know why God had chosen an infidel for this task, but who was he to question the wisdom of Allah. God moves in a mysterious way, but the Christians have no monopoly on faith.

But by the same token, I once saw a Somali slip from the back of a stationary truck that he had clambered onto. The fall was no more than seven or eight feet and he fell onto soft sand; but with the impact, his brittle thigh snapped like a matchstick.

*   *   *

And on the question of food, Jig-Jigga boasted an extraordinarily good restaurant. The entire European population consisted of the small governmental staff and four or five civilians, but there was a relatively large group of transients who passed through from time to time—truck drivers, mostly, on the long run from Mogadiscio to Harar, and most of whom made enough money, either by smuggling or by their legitimate pursuits, to demand good meals at the end of the dusty, lonely journey. For them, the town was in a favored position. The run up from Mogadiscio was a long and very dry one, through some of the most fearful country in the world. It was about eight hundred miles and eight days long—a hundred miles a day being a pretty good average out there. The powdery sand of the track and the sharp limestone of the rocky patches played

77

havoc on the tires, and it was generally reckoned that two complete sets were used up on a single two-way journey. Frequently, a ten-ton truck would arrive with its outer tires stuffed with grass in place of inner tubes, and this sort of traveling is hard on the toughest driver.

Once they had left Italian Somalia and had crossed into British Somaliland, the local tribes were more dangerous . . . and there was always trouble with the *shifta*. But as soon as the green hills that lay to the west of us hove in sight, they knew that they were coming close to Jig-Jigga, where there was water, and a marketplace, and pretty girls, and good drinks . . . and Armetta's.

Armetta's was a jumble of three beat-up old houses that had been joined together by the simple expedient of roofing over the space between them with straightened-out gasoline cans, planks, straw matting, thatch, whatever else was available. Each of the three houses had only two rooms, and the floors were of earth which had been hardened by frequent watering and brushings with a stiff broom. It lay, very handily, in the Street of the Brothels, which ran parallel to, and close by, the Street of the Butchers. There was a bead curtain over the main door to keep out the flies, and it wasn't the kind of place you would search for in the *Guide Michelin*.

But Armetta was an Italian, and if you give an Italian a roof over his head and some charcoal to cook on, you have the makings of a good restaurant. And Armetta's place was excellent.

Armetta himself was a big man, with a cheerful, suntanned face, a large paunch as befits a restaurateur, and a happy-go-lucky manner that was quite infectious. Most of his tables were outside, on the patio. But the tin roofing had been covered with creepers, and the walls were always flowering with bougainvillea and honeysuckle and sweet-smelling jasmine. Onions and tomatoes grew haphazardly all over the place, and there were jars of spices and bottles of wine, and homemade salami lying around like phallic emblems. And everywhere, all the time, there was music.

He was a great opera lover, and he owned Jig-Jigga's only phonograph. He had made it himself out of bits and pieces from a now-defunct Italian military store, using great ingenuity and a lot of patience. His records had come from Italy, and all that he required when his do-it-yourself project was done was some electricity.

For a while, he ran his phonograph on a cluster of batteries from ex-army Diesel trucks, but soon it occurred to him that if the town could not provide him with electricity, then he would provide it for the town. So, together with some cronies, he built a generator station, using, again, a couple of old army Diesel motors. At the end of a month he applied for, and received, a license to operate the town's electrical supply; everyone was charged five shillings a month for each light bulb he used, and the current was turned on at dusk, or whenever Armetta wanted to use his phonograph, which was most of the time.

The problem of ordering a meal there was not as it is in an ordinary restaurant. You sat down and chatted with Armetta or some of the girls for a while—the girls from the brothels used it as a kind of salon—or played chess with any driver who happened to be passing through; when you'd had enough to drink you'd ask Armetta if there was any food today, and Armetta would raise his eyebrows and say *"ma sicuro"* as if he didn't know that your chances of getting something to eat were actually about fifty-fifty—unless there were a lot of transients in town.

He'd ask what you felt like, and after a long discussion on food in general, he'd go off into the kitchen and start cooking. Once the lasagna, or the *past' asciuta,* or the ravioli were safely in preparation, he'd come back and renew the discussion, and

79

an hour or so later one of the girls would come in and say the food was ready. And whether it was midday or six in the evening, that was the end of the day's work, because after a session at Armetta's, the only possible next step was a good sleep.

And, all the while, he'd play his records—Gigli, and de Lucca, and Galli-Curci, and Tito Schippa, and Caniglia—all the greats of an era that has really gone by.

The girls would wander in and out, dressed in their bright "European" dresses made up by the local tailor out of colorful Indian prints, and there would be interminable arguments about everything under the sun. And you'd take time out to smell the jasmine and admire the tomatoes, and to savor the bouquet of a new batch of wine he'd just brought up from Djibouti. There was an air of *dolce far niente* that was quite admirable, and it was always a shame that sooner or later one had to do up one's belt and go back to the office.

* * *

The Street of the Brothels was not really called that, because none of the streets had any names at all. But since the Arab custom of grouping similar occupations together was followed here too, it was easy enough to locate a given point without a proper street name. If Suleiman Musa was a tailor, then without a doubt he lived and worked in the street where all the other tailors were. If you wanted to buy some meat, then you went to the only road where there were butchers' shops, where the meat would be hanging up in plain view, in complete carcasses, so that you simply said: "About five pounds or so ... off here," indicating the particular joint you wanted. There was a feeling of prestige involved in the buying of meat, because the Ethiopians—all the butchers, of course, were Ethiopian—somehow feel that the more meat a man eats, the better a man he is.

There were never any screens around these places, and dust and flies had free play; but it was not as bad as you might think. It was custom that food stores were painted blue, since blue distemper is unattractive to flies, and this system seems to work adequately by African standards if not by American. (Hospitals too, incidentally, are distempered blue almost everywhere in the Middle East, for the same reason.) And the butchers' shops always did a thriving trade. Meat, in all conscience, was cheap enough, as it is everywhere in Africa. The only refrigeration we had consisted of a few small kerosene refrigerators scattered about the station, most of them out of order and irreparable, so meat was always in great abundance because when you shot a buck it had to be eaten within two days; and a three-hundred-pound gerenuk provides a lot of good eating even when the meat is handed out free to whoever wants it.

* * *

We had a late lunch at Armetta's, Tafeta and I, and we chatted about nothing with some of the young girls and drank a great deal of wine, and I sent one of the girls to buy Armina's shawl for her, and when the sun was going down, throwing a red gold gleam over the distant Madar Pass, I climbed aboard the truck and set off once more on the long haul back to Dire-Daua.

7

The first crime of any consequence with which I personally had to deal was a complete and humiliating defeat.

Somebody stole a railway engine.

The railway, a single line running from Douanle on the border of French Somaliland clear up to Addis Ababa, was four hundred and fifty miles long; beyond the French border, it went on to Djibouti, and it is highly probable that the theft actually took place there, out of our jurisdiction.

But in the whole of the railway's length, there are only four sidings, two of them disused, and no auxiliary lines whatsoever.

The general manager of the railway administration, an Englishman from British Railways in England, came to see me one morning with the incredible news that one of his engines, somewhere en route from Addis Ababa to Dire-Daua for overhaul, had simply disappeared. It had been flagged through Akaki, Ada, Mojjo, and Hadama, the first four villages on the way down from the capital; had taken on water at Awash; had passed through Miesso, Baroda, and Afdam; and thereafter had not been seen by anybody.

Between Afdam and Dire-Daua there is only one small stop, Gota, and between Dire-Daua and Douanle there are six more—El Bah, Mello, Waruf, Addagallah, Sarman, and Aisha—and to all of these stations, signals had been sent asking for news of the missing locomotive, with no results at all. Most of the stations had a small police post of sorts, usually in the charge of a Sergeant or Corporal, so I sent off a few signals too, and learned that the disappearance had apparently occurred on the Baroda-Afdam section of the line; roughly speaking, in the territory that my old friend Ras Matara called his own. But in that section there are no sidings at all, no disused stretches of line, nothing on which a locomotive could be shunted, and it occurred to me that Matara himself could not possibly find any use for such a cumbersome piece of machinery even if he could get it off the line, which he patently couldn't.

At the end of four days, every mile of the line had been searched, and there was still no sign of the engine; it had simply vanished.

I spoke to Seyoum about it. Seyoum was one of the older Ethiopian officers, an ungainly, awkwardly built man with a huge set of teeth that made him look almost exactly like a black Fernandel. He said: "I think someone is trying to get Ras Matara into trouble, hoping he'll be blamed for it."

"But how the hell did they get it off the track, can you tell me that?"

He shook his head. "It has to be over the border, in French Somaliland, it can't be anywhere else."

"Then why didn't it pass through all those stations down the line? It didn't even pass through Dire-Daua, where they were standing out on the tracks waiting for it."

He shook his head and said stubbornly: "It's in French Somaliland somewhere, it must be, the only part of the line we can't search."

I sent off a signal to the French Chief of Police in Djibouti, and asked if I might pay him a courtesy visit, and meanwhile went up to Addis Ababa to see if I could find out anything there. I had intended sending a Superintendent, but the Governor said: "Good God, it makes us look such idiots! You'd better go yourself, see if the Ethiopians on the other side have any ideas."

"The Emperor's people?"

"Yes, Colonel Banks, he's head of their police."

At this time, the Ethiopian army was British-trained, their police force British-officered. Later, the Swedes took over when we became suddenly unpopular, and then the Russians, and then the Danes—all by invitation of the Emperor himself, who has always been aware of his country's need for Western help and advice.

I ordered out the sybaritic personal coach again, and went up to the capital.

*   *   *

Addis Ababa, the New Flower, sprawls untidily over the top of a mountain more than eight thousand feet high. It is a town of color and contrast, where the rich black soil and torrential but regular rainfall ensure a never-ending succession of flowers, shrubs, and fruit. Roses are in abundance everywhere. There is the ubiquitous hibiscus side by side with rhododendron, and morning-glory and honeysuckle are spread in wild confusion. There are fine old-fashioned hotels, short on the civilized amenities such as plumbing, but very long indeed on the cultural amenities such as service. In the whole of Africa, of course, the ancient art of serving is an honorable and efficiently practical profession, but nowhere does it reach more comfortable heights than in Addis Ababa.

It has only been the capital since 1896, and before its "westernizing" by the great Emperor Menelik II, was little more than a village. Even today its population is not much more than two hundred thousand, and its first automobiles were imported as recently as 1924, after the Emperor's first visit to Europe, but it manages to be a bustling and thriving place, though the casual visitor often wonders just why it should be there; its industries merely support its own population.

Its western aspect is reflected in its bars and cafés and restaurants, where twenty different nationalities sip their French drinks, served by Greek waiters, to the sound of Italian orchestras. And outside the town, in the beautiful eucalyptus forests (which Menelik planted) the "foreign quarters" are really the busiest in the whole of Africa.

Our Superintendent there, Michael Evans, was sick with some kind of fever, which I thought might have been brought on by boredom, so I packed him off on the train back to Dire-Daua for a week's rest, leaving the post in charge of the capable Ethiopian staff, and went into town to see Colonel Banks.

Evans had told me that he had not left the railway area since shortly after his arrival, when, attempting a night on the town, he had been brusquely ordered back to his own territory by some of the Emperor's police; but no one seemed to bother when I strolled into the city and made my way up the steep hill to police headquarters. I was wearing the E.R.A.P. badge on my safari hat, and was conscious that the only police patrol I passed on the way there stared at it with a great deal of interest; I also remembered that the British officers who ran the Emperor's police force disapproved of us very considerably.

It is quite astonishing how partisan the normally nonpolitical Englishman can become at times. (A similar case in point is that of the British police in Palestine; when the country changed hands, in 1947, some of the resigning British police went over to the Arabs and some to the Israelis, and thenceforth fought each other with all the weapons at their disposal.) I wondered what sort of reception I would receive.

But the Commandant, Colonel Banks, was affable and courteous. He was a tall, white-haired man of impressive good looks, rather like the Hollywood idea of a European diplomat. If he was aware that protocol was being broken by my presence there, he showed no discomfort.

I said: "In theory, at least, I'm not supposed to wander about your town, am I? Not more than twenty feet from the railway line, isn't it?"

"Good heavens," he said, "don't worry about that. No one's going to arrest you. If they do, then I'll hear about it and come and get you out. Only don't get into any sort of trouble, will you? It could be very embarrassing."

I said: "Michael Evans at the railway station appears to have been harassed a little. No one lets him come into town, and he's bored stiff with looking at locomotives and repair sheds."

"Well, that's not very nice, is it?" He leaned back in his chair and put his feet up, and said: "A hangover from the last administration, they weren't very popular. Tell him that he's free to come and go as he pleases. Only that's quite unofficial, and I mustn't be quoted."

"Did you hear about our missing locomotive?"

He started laughing. "I heard. Have you found it?"

"No. It's just vanished."

"At Baroda, I hear. That's Ras Matara's territory."

"Even if he had the means for getting it off the line, which he hasn't, what the hell would he do with a damn great locomotive in the middle of the bush?"

"Yes, I rather wondered about that myself. Well, it's your problem, not mine, I'm happy to say. Is that the reason for your visit? Delighted to see you, of course."

"Not really. My Ethiopian officers seem to feel that your Ethiopian officers hate their guts. They signed on with us willingly enough, but no one thought the occupation of the Reserved Areas would last for more than a few months and it was a chance for them to get taken on, eventually, by the Emperor. But it's been five years now, and I have the idea there's a certain odium between the two forces. I wondered what we could do to improve things."

He thought a long time before answering. He said slowly: "Yes, I'd like to see a better relationship. There must be something more we can do, if we're both willing."

"A temporary exchange of officers, perhaps?"

"Oh, no. His Majesty would never agree. But perhaps . . . I hear you have a very good hockey team down there."

We had indeed. The Dire-Daua Police Hockey Team was supposedly the best in the country. I said: "A match? On our ground, or yours?"

He said gently: "We can't really allow your people here unless you make the first gesture. So why don't you invite us down there? I'm sure Sir Reginald would approve, he's very much in favor of smoothing things out."

"I'm sure he will. All right, I'll arrange it. Some time next week?"

"Good. Only . . ." He hesitated. "The railway is yours, of course, and we don't really have the money to spare, not to bring down a whole team . . ."

"I'll have a word with the railway administration. I'm sure they can rustle up some free passes."

"Splendid. You'll forgive me if I don't come myself? We mustn't appear too enthusiastic."

"Of course. Will you come and have dinner with me to-night? Or would that be too enthusiastic too?"

He said regretfully: "As a matter of fact, I'm rather tied up just now. The police force hasn't been paid for three months, and now the local petrol suppliers have cut off our fuel because we haven't paid them for quite a while. I'm dining with the manager of the Shell Company to see if we can't at least get mobile again."

I was astounded. "But . . . but why on earth not? Where's all the money?"

He shrugged. "It will come in the course of time. It's sometimes a little late here, you know."

"And you haven't been paid for three months?"

"In my own case, a little more than that."

"Then why do you stay, for God's sake?"

He said gently: "Because I like it here."

"Well, that's a good enough reason. What is there to like so much?"

"You'll find out. Where do you come from?"

"Oh, Cairo, Jerusalem, the Sudan . . . that sort of thing."

"You'll find these people very different from the Arabs."

"I'd noticed that already."

He went on: "The aristocrats of Africa. They regard the Arabs as slave traders, and the Swahilis as slaves. An ancient race with all the dignity and self-assurance that only a long heritage can provide." He was getting quite chauvinistic. He said suddenly: "What are the qualities you admire most? In men, I mean?"

"Oh, I don't know . . . in the abstract, I suppose . . . Hell, that's a difficult question."

"Is it courage? The Ethiopian is the bravest man on earth. You'll find that out one day, and you'll be glad of it too. Is it honesty? Well, there are thieves here, just as there are anywhere else in the world. But here, at least in some parts, they still cut off their hands as a deterrent, that's how much they hate thievery. Is it loyalty? Wait till you've made a few friends; you'll find out about loyalty . . ."

"What about bribery? They say there's quite a lot of that about. I'm not arguing the point, of course . . ."

"Bribery? Of course there is. Plenty. More than you might find in some other places. But don't you see, money has such little importance for them—it's just a handy thing to have around, that's all. Besides, if you've lived in Egypt, don't say you expect to find no corruption."

"I know. It's just a point. Do you have any other problems to iron out with us?"

"No, I don't think so. That hockey match, it should be a very good thing. Another step in the right direction."

"I hope so."

"You will remember, won't you, that this has been a very . . . unofficial visit? We're not supposed to admit that you exist, you know how it is. And I'm really sorry I can't join you for dinner. Do you have any particular plans?"

"No. I thought I'd just look around for a while."

"Try the Olympia, it's an excellent place. Good cabaret, great orchestra, all that sort of thing."

"I will. And thank you for your help."

He stood up and walked with me to the door.

"Do you want any addresses?"

"I'll manage. Thanks all the same."

He held out his hand and said wistfully: "Give my regards to Sir Reginald. I'd very much like to meet him, but of course . . ."

"A fantasy, isn't it? I was never very good at protocol."

He said: "It's a question of . . . of *face*. We have to pretend all the time, but if we didn't . . . we'd be at each other's throats, so perhaps it makes sense after all. Where will you sleep tonight?"

"Don't worry about it, I've got my own coach on the train, in *our* territory."

He smiled. "Yes, of course. Well, have a good time. It's a great place, Addis Ababa."

"Good-night. And thank you."

I dined at the Olympia that night, as Colonel Banks had suggested.

The waiters were Greek, the cuisine French, and the orchestra Italian. I danced with a very attractive young girl who spoke, like Armina, kitchen Italian, and who said everyone called her Registri, short for *registri d'organo*, organ stops. She laughed and indicated her eyes, which were huge, and round, and black. After our second dance, while we were making cheerful conversation in a mixture of French and Italian, she left me to join a visiting chieftain, a *Ras*, who had come to see the sights.

He was a startling sight, the *Ras*. He stood in the doorway for a moment, staring at the orchestra, at the starched white tablecloths, and at the glittering chandelier. Then he strode to a table, sat down, clapped his hands, and ordered food and wine. A bandolier was slung across his chest, and he was dressed in a khaki uniform of jodhpurs and bush jacket, with puttees and broad leather sandals. His bodyguards, three soldiers in a similar uniform, sat on the floor beside him with their rifles (British army Lee-Enfields) slung across their knees. Every time the *Ras* took out a cigarette, one of the soldiers leaped to his feet and lit it for him, and then sat down again. Once, the *Ras* pulled a leg off the roast guinea hen he was eating and handed it to one of the soldiers.

The waiters showed no sign of alarm and indeed stepped over the bodyguards with a well-practiced agility which made me think it was a fairly common occurrence. The juxtaposition of the very traditional and the very modern, of the bush and the city, was fascinating.

He was watching the girl called Organ Stops, and after he had finished his meal he signaled her imperiously, and she whispered to me: *"Scusa,* he wants to make love."

She went over and sat with him for a while, and drank a lot of *tej,* and then they left together. When they returned, an hour or so later, the *Ras* ordered another dinner and some more *tej,* and the girl came back to my table and we took up where we had left off. It was all very charming and delightful.

* * *

The hockey match was arranged about a week after my visit to the capital. It was to be quite an event. Among our own men it was construed as the first sign that the "real" Ethiopians were relenting toward them. Of course, they had joined our police force with the express consent of their government, but nonetheless, as time dragged on and the Reserved Areas remained reserved, their position vis-à-vis the rest of their countrymen was getting a little strained.

We bought an ox to celebrate the occasion, and we borrowed the field in the garrison of the King's African Rifles. It was a proper hockey field, more or less correctly marked out with newly painted white lines, and it had a wooden stand along one side that would hold several hundred people on its lower benches; the upper benches were not considered safe enough to sit on, but they looked very impressive.

We ran a very good team. It was made up of three or four of the more agile British officers, headed by the Governor, who was captain, two Somalis who were included in the team for political purposes—to point to the fact that the area included a large number of Somalis—and the rest were Ethiopians, both officers and constables.

The night before the game there was a party in the Mess Hall at which the ox was killed and served raw to the men while it was still warm and steaming, and in our own Mess we entertained the Ethiopian officers who had come down with their team, and any other passersby who happened to need an excuse for a party. Consequently, when the game was due to begin, no one was even up; the Adjutant had thoughtlessly arranged it for ten o'clock in the morning. So we rearranged it for the late afternoon.

The weather was wonderful; a mild cool breeze blew across the sandy green of the field, and the sun was pleasantly hot. I was included in the team for reasons of courtesy, although I had never played hockey before coming here. It was very pleasant running all over the field and taking an occasional swipe at the ball when it came my way, and indeed, I was instrumental in the scoring of a goal by the other side.

Two of us were racing toward the ball from opposite directions, the other man being one of our junior officers who was supposed to be the best player on the field, and also the fastest sprinter; it was Inspector Clifton, and he weighed perhaps a hundred and forty pounds. At this time, I weighed just over a hundred and eighty. The inevitable collision between us came right in front of our goal. I was moving forward at a creditable rate, considering the party the previous night, and Clifton was streaking toward me with the speed of light, and we met head on; or rather, stomach on. He bounced off me, and as he fell I saw the look of utter consternation on his face; he must have shot more than twenty feet through the air before he landed on his back, and the sound could have been heard half a mile away. The ball, lost in the melee, trickled into our own goal, the defense at the time being doubled up with laughter. A great cheer went up from the crowd on the sidelines, and it occurred to me that an apology to our captain, His Excellency the Governor, was called for.

I walked over to where he stood grinning at me, and told him I was sorry.

"Don't worry," he whispered, "we were leading, you know. Now we're even again, and that's how it should be."

Catching the look on my face, he said: "It's got to be a draw. Didn't I tell you?"

"Oh. I see. Yes, of course."

But the star of the game was a young baboon called Susan.

Susan was the pet of one of the K.A.R. officers. She lived in their Mess, and always followed the local athletics with the greatest interest. It seemed that she had a certain contempt for us poor humans when it came to so wild a sport as chasing a ball over the field, and she had, in the past, frequently joined in the game when she got loose from her chain.

On this occasion, just as the visitors were making a massed attack on our goal, Susan broke loose, leaped down from the stand, and dashed across the field after the ball.

I was sitting on the sidelines at the moment, recovering from a burst of energy which had left me breathless, and as she passed me I made a swipe at her with my stick, since it occurred to me that although we were used to Susan, the visitors were not. But I missed, and in no time at all she had seized the ball and was haring off across the field with it, hotly pursued by most of the players. This, of course, was the worst thing they could have done.

There was a properly established procedure when this sort of thing happened, as it did quite frequently. We had found that once Susan got the ball, the only thing to do was to sit down and take a rest; in a short time, Susan would then become disgruntled and wander off the field, chewing at the ball and making her way back to her master for sympathy. He would then recover the ball for us, and we would get up and get on with the game.

But the visitors knew nothing about this, and also took their game a little more seriously than we did, so they chased the poor bewildered baboon in an effort to catch her and recover the ball themselves.

The game at once took on something of the aspect of a Mack Sennet comedy. There was a Corporal in the lead, and it soon became a personal duel between the two of them. As Susan sped from one end of the field to the other, turning at times to hurl insults at her tormentor, we all became immersed in the academic question, Could a man outrun a baboon or not? One by one the other pursuers dropped out to watch the Corporal.

He was incredibly fast, moving across the sunbaked field like a leopard, from one end to the other and back again, the gray dust spurting up from under his bare feet in little clouds, and at last, Susan could stand no more of the indignity. She stopped in her tracks, turned and waited till the Corporal was almost on her, then hurled the ball straight at him. It was the fastest thing I have ever seen; he dropped to the ground in a flash and the missile went hurtling over his head. There was a spontaneous cheer from the crowd; the Corporal picked himself up, and Susan went leaping back to her place among the spectators, crying with chagrin and looking for sympathy.

We went on with the game. As the Governor had decided, it ended in a draw.

There was a celebration again that night. We had beer and raw meat at a huge bare wooden table in the barracks, and when the long meal was over, the Ehiopians took it in turn to stand on the table and chant of their victories over lion and leopard, of the battles they had fought, and of the women they had loved. As they sang, the rest of us listened attentively or shouted encouragement.

Toward two in the morning, we ran out of beer, so the Duty Officer took the truck into town and opened up one of the stores and came back with a new supply, and the Ethiopians prized off the caps with their strong white teeth and swore that next time Addis Ababa would beat the hell out of us.

And at half past five in the morning, the police force strag-gled back to its duty.

It was cool and still and quiet outside in the early dawn, and the opposing team slept in the barracks for a while and then went back to the capital on the afternoon train. And when we went up there for the return match a week later they trounced us horribly.

We should have taken Susan along with us.

8

I was dining alone at the Café Cloudot one night, eating roast partridge and drinking beer, when the Duty Officer, Inspector Gabre, came to find me with news of a minor calamity.

In retrospect, it seems to me that most of our time out there was spent on trivial matters, and any modern, western police force would, I am sure, regard our approach to police work as pure *opera buffa*. But the circumstances precluded any serious approach, even if a more earnest attitude had been desirable, which it wasn't.

The café was also an open-air cinema, and Gabre didn't like to interrupt *La Grande Illusion*, which was on the screen under the trees; he said, whispering: "We might be having a little diplomatic trouble at the station, sir. Mr. Berren has arrested Maria Teslata, the Duke of Harar's young lady."

"Oh my God. Whatever for?"

"He's charging her now. Assault on a police officer. You might want to come round and see what you can do. She's being rather violent."

"Oh, for God's sake. Sit down and tell me what happened."

He pulled up a chair and said: "Well, she was at the cinema, and got into a fight with two Somali women, and these things can get out of hand, you know, so the manager called in the policeman outside, and the policeman called in Mr. Berren. It seems that she . . . well, she attacked him."

"You mean she hit him? He was probably rude to her, it serves him right."

"No, not quite. He was trying to drag her off one of these Somali girls, she was trying to kill her, and Maria . . . well, she took hold of Mr. Berren's testicles with both hands, and pulled, hard. He says it was extremely painful."

"Oh. What about the fight?"

"That's all over. As soon as he got Maria out, it just simmered down, and they went on with the show."

"And the Duke, presumably, is not there?"

"No, sir. He has a meeting tonight with the Italian Trucking Company, the Sabena Company, he sent her to the cinema alone."

"Well, we'd better do something about it before he finds out, hadn't we? That bloody Berren, he ought to have more sense."

Berren was a rather stolid young man, good-looking, a bit overzealous, and a very recent arrival from England. All the new arrivals from London had been briefed there, at my insistence, on the importance of maintaining a good relationship with our host country even if it meant bending all the rules a bit.

I went round to the station with Gabre, a few minutes' walk up the road, and was shocked to see the state Inspector Berren was in. He was sitting on a chair in his office, clutching at his groin, his face white as an aspirin.

I said:"My God, are you going to be all right?"

He nodded unhappily. "Yes, sir, I think so. That . . . that bitch!"

"That's no way to talk to His Highness' concubine. Do you want to see a doctor?"

"No, I'll be all right in a while. It hurts to stand up, that's all. It hurts a lot."

There was no sign of Maria, and I asked where she was. He said: "Cell number three."

"And you've made all the necessary entries in the books?"

"Yes, sir, I have."

I said: "Well, tear them out. I'm going to release her. And if this gets to the Governor's ears, he's going to deport you."

He said, pained in more ways than one: "But she attacked me! She grabbed hold of my balls with both hands, put a foot in my stomach, and yanked, hard."

I said: "Her privilege. I don't care what she did to you, we just don't want to rock the boat, that's all. It's a very touchy situation."

Gabre had solemnly produced the prison entry record, and the charge sheet in triplicate, and Berren, resignedly, doctored the books with a couple of torn-out pages while I went off to see Maria.

Number three was the best of our cells, with a large barred window overlooking the trees in the courtyard; a highly scented *frangi-pani*, with huge white and yellow blossoms, was right up against it, and the air inside was sickly sweet. The only other prisoner there was an elderly Galla woman who had beaten her husband half to death with a cooking pot. There was no furniture of any sort, and the Galla woman sat patiently on the floor, a blanket around her, staring at the young, fashionably dressed half-Italian girl who stood sullenly in the corner, glowering.

I said cheerfully: "Well, I never expected to meet you here, Maria."

She said, furious: "Wait till Harar hears about this . . ."

I said: "That's exactly what I was about to say to you. Only I was going to offer not to tell him about it."

She stared, and I said, pushing her: "My God, you come down into *our* territory, you start a fight in a cinema full of people, with Somalis for God's sake, you beat up one of my officers who was very correctly trying to stop a riot from starting . . . My God, if Harar hears about it, or even Sir Reginald . . . We've got the makings of an international incident on our hands, haven't we? Where do you think that will leave you?"

She said sullenly: "Harar will take care of me."

"But it's going to be very embarrassing for him, isn't it?"

She was a very bright young woman. She said, her temper suddenly gone: "Does that mean you're letting me out of here?"

"Of course. That's exactly what it means. Have you had your dinner?"

"Yes, I have."

"So come and have a drink with me. What time are you meeting the Duke?"

"Soon after midnight. He told me to wait at the Café Cloudot."

"Good, that's where I'm eating. Come and watch the rest of the show with me, and we'll wait for him."

"All right." She looked suddenly at Gabre and said: "Tell that idiot Berren, tell him I said he couldn't hold me here."

Gabre was all smiles, holding open the cell door for us, and we went back to the Cloudot and watched the rest of the film.

Harar turned up at a quarter to one, and slid in beside us and said, smiling broadly: "I hear you had a little trouble tonight."

I should have known he'd have been told, one way or another. I nodded, and he said: "All over now?"

99

"All over. No problems."

"Good." He was holding Maria's hand, and she was smiling gently at him, a lovely, cool, controlled young lady once again. It was very hard not to feel paternalistic about her.

We sat around, talking and drinking till five o'clock, and then there was all the fuss again getting his car started.

I said: "It's time you had this car fixed up properly, can't Sabena do it for you?"

He grimaced. "They're getting me a new motor from Italy, God knows when it will get here." He shot out his hand. "No hard feelings about that *fracas?*"

"No, of course not."

"I mean, you won't try and keep us out of Dire-Daua?"

"You think I could if I wanted to?"

"No, I don't suppose so."

"And when are you going to invite me up to Harar?"

"Any time. The palace is yours."

"I'll take you up on that."

I watched them drive off together up the street in the early light, and when he was well up on the tortuous road that led to the walled city of Harar on the top, I could still hear the old motor coughing and spitting as it wound its way through the lonely, deserted mountain.

I went home to bed for three hours' sleep before the day's work should once more begin.

*   *   *

There was an angry argument going on at the steps to the police station when I arrived at eight o'clock. A highly excited Ethiopian woman was clutching a bottle of cloudy milk in one hand, and dragging a small Danakil girl with the other, and Seyoum was trying to calm them down. The child was crying, rubbing a bony fist into her eyes, pulling back hard and falling over her dress, an old ragged shift that was open down to her naked waist, her tiny, pointed breasts just budding.

The woman waved the bottle at me and shouted, and Seyoum said laconically: "She's decided she doesn't want any more sand in her milk, she thinks the police should do something about it."

I sat down on the wall and watched them for a while, and they calmed down soon, and Seyoum said patiently: "The girl is a milkmaid, she delivers bottles of milk around town, at the controlled price, ten cents a bottle."

The bottles were old beer bottles, collected one way or another at the garrison of the King's African Rifles or from the bars in town. I never did find out just who it was controlled the price of milk, but somewhere there was an ordinance that said the maximum price was ten cents.

Seyoum said: "Most of the time, she waters it down to make it go further, and the well in her parents' house is not a very good one, so the water's all sandy."

I took the bottle and looked at it. The milk was a dull gray color, the color of bad *tej*. The child spoke no Italian, so I talked to her through Seyoum, and said: "You know you're not supposed to put dirty water in milk, don't you?"

She said promptly: "Then let them pay more for it."

"No. The law says ten cents."

"Ten cents is for dirty milk, if you want it clean you have to pay more."

I asked Seyoum: "Is that a fair price? If it's not, can we do anything about it?"

He shrugged. "It's too much. Town prices."

"All right then." I found ten cents in my pocket and gave it to the little girl, and said: "Now you run off and find the lady a bottle of clean milk." She looked at me, beaming suddenly, and said: "Where do you get *your* milk?"

Nine years old and a saleswoman already.

I said: "At the store. Why, do you want another customer?"

"Yes. I bring you milk every morning."

"All right. You know where I live?"

"I know. Twenty cents a bottle."

"Ten cents."

"But you don't want dirty milk, you're the policeman, you must have clean milk. Twenty cents a bottle."

I said, not feeling I could cope with her very well: "Inspector Seyoum will pay you, so you argue with him about it, all right?"

"All right." She ran off, clutching the coin I had given her, and I called after her to remind her about the fresh bottle. She paid no heed at all, and the old woman looked at me accusingly and said: "A Danakil child! If she had been an Ethiopian, you wouldn't have been so good to her. She should go to prison!"

Seyoum looked at me, grinned, and shepherded her out.

And everyday thereafter, the little girl came round to the house at six o'clock in the morning, and left a bottle of milk. It was usually fairly clean, though I never did find out how much we were paying for it.

*　　*　　*

This was the time I acquired my first cheetahs, the first of many.

I found a Danakil tribesman wandering through the town with two little cubs, no more than a few days old, in a basket on his arm, looking for a buyer. I was with Sergeant Dana at the time—a skinny, easy-going bushman who had come in from one of the outlying posts, a tall and very attractive man whose affability hid an almost frightening strength. There was a legend about him to the effect that his post had been attacked, a few months before, by a band of Somali *shifta* who had broken in during the night and stolen the four rifles that were there. Dana had been in one of the village brothels at the

102

time, and on his return to his post, he had tracked the maraud-ing band down, alone, and had killed all nine of them with his service revolver. His report on the incident was in the files, and the last line read: "and the stolen rifles, of course, were immedi-ately recovered."

Now, the two tiny cubs were snarling and hissing, their fur still unspotted, their needle teeth tearing at everything that came near them, and when I asked the Danakil what he wanted for them and was told one Maria Theresa dollar each —or about seventy-five cents—I bought them both, over Dana's strong protests; he said that in his part of the world he could get me all the cheetahs I could possibly want, for pennies apiece.

Cheetahs make attractive pets, become very affectionate, and their marked territorial imperative makes them good watchdogs—they dislike intruders and show their anger visibly.

A little later on, I acquired a fully grown one, and although cheetahs are usually extremely gentle, this one was as savage as a leopard. And small wonder, it had been monstrously mis-treated.

One of the Italians who lived in the town, a storekeeper named Bonelli, had bought it from an itinerant trader in the hope that it might serve as a watchdog, which indeed it did; the whole quarter was terrified of it. It was already fully grown, and had been caught by the time-honored tradition of being run down to the point of exhaustion and then merely picked up. But Bonelli had not the patience for the kind of loving care that training demands, and had tried to beat it into submission, and it had consequently grown more and more savage. It was wild, unpredictable, and a danger to the whole area; more importantly, perhaps, it was being savagely treated by a misera-ble man who had no business owning animals at all.

It was reported to me in the course of conversation with one of the local policemen that Bonelli had broken a walking stick across the cheetah's back, so I went over to see him, threatened him with a jail sentence, and finally bought it off him for five Maria Theresa dollars.

In the safety of my house, I put a collar on him, tied a rope to the collar, and fastened the other end of the rope to a heavy log, so that he could move around freely but not too fast. And in the space of a month of careful feeding and attention, I had him relatively tame. But only relatively. Frequently, while I was fondling him (he would purr loudly like a contented cat), he would suddenly lash out with his sharp front claws. My clothes were torn to shreds, one pair of pants after another, and my arms and legs were permanently scarred; but a cheetah's claws are feline (unlike a lion's or leopard's, which hold rotten carrion in their concave undersizes and are therefore highly poisonous) and quite clean, so this was never any problem.

In time, my fondness for him became reciprocal. I called him Satan, and he would prowl the garden or the house on the end of his twenty-foot rope, dragging his log along when he felt like it, and at night would sleep contentedly on my bed, across my feet, snarling angrily every time I moved.

He was a splendid animal, and after the first month or two, he would wait for me on the veranda every time I came home from work, would leap up to my shoulders like a dog, and play for five minutes or so before suddenly losing his temper again and ruining yet another pair of trousers. And he lorded it over the other two cheetahs, now named Napoleon and Josephine, like a despot, not letting them eat until he had finished eating, not letting them into the bedroom at night, which was all very proper and the way it should be. Age and physical strength still command respect in the bush.

But before Satan's arrival, when I just had the two cubs, there was the problem of house training, which is an almost impossible task with cheetahs; they just go when they have to, wherever they might be. So I took them round to the office,

Sergeant Dana still protesting and promising to find me a hundred more, and put them in the In tray on my desk, which, to tell the truth, was not very often used.

And while I was contemplating them happily, watching them tumble over each other like small, energetic kittens, I heard the most appalling scream come from the garage which stood just behind my office. It was partly a scream of pain, and partly a yell of furious anger. I looked at Dana and ran for the door, and bumped into Sharma, the Indian Chief Clerk, as he too ran from his office to see what the trouble was. The three of us hurried down to the garage, and there was Inspector Seyoum, at the big iron vise on the workbench, turning the handle like an old-time inquisitor.

On his back on the floor, both ankles in the vise, was one of the constables, still yelling his head off as Seyoum applied more and more pressure on the two iron jaws.

Seyoum stopped when he saw me, stood stiffly to attention, saluted, and said quickly: "Dirty boots on parade, sir."

I couldn't believe my ears. For a moment, I was unable to say anything, even if I could have made myself heard over the screaming of the constable. Seyoum hit the bar with his fist and spun it loose, and the man got up painfully from the floor, stood to attention, and saluted too, and for a moment the tableau held.

Seyoum felt it was time to say something again, and he said quickly: "Constable Makenno, sir, dirty boots on parade, the second time this week."

It was an extraordinary point of honor among the Ethiopians that they were, without a doubt, the smartest constabulary force on the Continent. They would spend long hours with flat pieces of bone, working on the leather of their boots and belts till they shone like glass. Their khaki uniforms were always stiff and highly starched, and ironed by the women they brought into their barracks to a peak of perfection which I had never before encountered. Even on patrol, even down in the dry gray dust of the riverbed, they would keep the shine there by the frequent use of a pocket handkerchief or a piece of clean rag they carried for the purpose. And each company vied with all the others for superiority in the matter of smartness on patrol.

The six a.m. parade, which was a combination of inspection, lecture, and duty roster, with some old-fashioned drill thrown in to keep them on their toes, was always a remarkable event, witnessed by any passersby who happened to be around at that hour of the morning, and was an occasion for each man to show off his immaculate appearance; it was also an opportunity for each Inspector to show that his company was the smartest in the Reserved Areas.

I said to Seyoum, quite patiently: "His boots are not clean, so you're breaking his ankles?"

"Not breaking them, sir. Just a little pressure to make him remember."

I said: "If I catch you doing that again, I'll fire you, understand?"

"Yes, sir."

I said to Makenno: "And if I ever catch you with dirty boots on parade, I'll fire you too. Now get back to work, both of you."

Seyoum saluted again, turned smartly on his heel, and was gone. Makenno limped off painfully, but he was playing hockey that evening, so he hadn't been seriously hurt.

Perhaps that is not true; the Ethiopians' resistance to pain is phenomenal . . .

My driver, a few days later, asked permission to take what he called "some time off" in order to see the doctor; he had tonsilitis, and there were three or four local doctors in town, as well as our own, an Italian who was actually a veterinarian, but served as station M.O.

I said I'd make an appointment with the M.O. for him, but

he shook his head, and said: "No need, sir, my cousin is a doctor, too."

He went off for an operation, but within the hour I found him sitting patiently in the car, waiting for me. I said: "I thought you were going to have your tonsils out?"

He nodded, opened his mouth wide, to show me the bloody mess at the back of his throat, and said, grinning: "All finished, sir, no more tonsilitis, no more tonsils."

One hour . . . I discovered how the operation took place. The "doctor" merely gave him a loop of string to swallow, pulled it back up with the tonsils nicely hooked on, and snipped them off with a pair of scissors. No anesthetic, no disinfectant; and no time wasted.

I said: "My God, it must have hurt like hell."

He shrugged. "Little bit, not too much." He was still swallowing hard to keep the blood off his immaculate uniform.

* * *

And then, in the early evening, Inspector Berren came in, apparently quite recovered from his defeat at the hands of Maria. Berren was slowly taking over what little there was of our Criminal Investigation Department.

He said cheerfully: "Well, we've got a murder on our hands, I thought you ought to know about it, the *Khadis* are raising hell."

The *Khadis* were the Somali Holy Men, the priests, and it was a convenience, in this town that was ninety percent Ethiopian, to let the Somali Tribal Council, known as the Khadis' Court, handle any matters that had any tribal overtones at all. We kept an eye on their proceedings to avoid any reversion to the old excesses of the bush, but otherwise left them more or less alone.

He put a file on my desk and said: "It's been going on for some time, apparently, a man named Issa Daoudi. He just murdered his brother, a quarrel over camels."

"So what's been going on for some time? And why shouldn't the Khadis' Court handle it?"

He said: "Well, there's no real proof that Issa committed the murder, though he's been boasting about it to the wrong people, and the *Khadis* want to burn him for it."

"Oh."

It was a relatively common punishment among the Somalis who lived on the edge of civilization. They would tie an offender's hands together, bind them in gasoline-soaked rags, and set fire to them. I looked through the file and told Berren to sit down and tell me about it.

He said: "Three weeks ago, he told the court that his brother, Mahmoud, was making arrow poison. Strychnine."

"Is he a Mitgan? One of the untouchables?"

"No, sir, he is not."

"They're the only people who make arrow poison."

"Yes, I know that."

Arrow poison, though used freely in the bush, was outlawed in the towns, where it could not be put to any useful purpose, but every Somali knew how to make it. They would take the bark and the roots of the *strychnos psilosperum* shrub, shave it with their daggers into long thin slivers, and boil it with water in an earthenware vessel, letting it simmer for days on end, crouching over the thorn-root fire on their haunches, poking at the brew with a thin stick, watching it as carefully as a skilled chef with a boeuf bourguignon. When it reached just the right consistency, they would then pour it into a large crab shell to dry out, and at the end of two days, the resulting paste, looking like a mixture of shoe polish and spaghetti sauce, was a fast and extremely deadly poison. They would test it by nicking the ear of a goat—preferably a neighbor's goat—and if the animal lived longer than a minute or so, they would throw away the batch and make a new one.

Berren said: "For some weeks now, Issa has been telling the *Khadi* that his brother was making poison and intended to murder him. The *Khadis* made inquiries and found out that it just wasn't true. But last night, the brother died, and his wife found a shellfull of poison beside him, and a spearhead which had been dipped in it; the brother had a small cut on his left hand, the kind of cut he might have made accidentally while he was coating his blades. Now Issa is saying, very piously, that he knew all along something like this would happen."

"So how come it's murder?"

Berren shrugged: "Issa told his wife what had really happened. Having planted the seed in the Khadis' Court, having warned them that his brother was messing around with strychnine, he went over to his brother's place last night, hit him over the head and knocked him out, planted the bowl of poison there, smeared some of it onto Mahmoud's spearhead, and then punctured the skin of his hand with it. End of Mahmoud. Unfortunately, the wife told her boyfriend, who happens to be a scribe at the Khadis' Court. So the whole plot was blown wide open, all the brilliance wasted because Issa couldn't keep his fool mouth shut. Now he's denying the whole thing, but the *Khadis* believe what the scribe told them, and they want to burn his hands off, teach him a lesson. And so, Issa has turned himself in to us, knowing his chances with us are a lot better."

"I see. Are we ever going to be able to prove a case?"

"No, sir, not a hope."

"Have you arrested him?"

"I thought I'd better talk to you about it first. This time."

He was still smarting from the Maria Teslata affair.

"Well, don't. I suppose we'd never get a deposition from the wife?"

"No, sir. She denies she even knows the scribe, let alone that she told him of Issa's boasting. She has to, doesn't she, or she's in trouble with them for adultery. Besides, she's run off, gone back to her tribe in the desert somewhere, out of our territory. She's afraid that Issa will kill her, either for talking out of turn, or for having a lover. Or for both."

"A family feud—you don't believe we can stop it just by locking him up, do you?"

"Well, at least until he gets out."

"And if we can't prove a case, we've got to let him go, haven't we? Any other brothers in the family?"

"Four. Only one of them in Dire-Daua, two in Jig-Jigga, and one up in Awash, working at the watering station there."

"Any chance one of them will take up the vendetta and kill off Issa?"

"I'd say a very good chance. If we arrest him, we've got to bring him to trial within fourteen days. Even if we get a continuance, and keep on getting continuances, we'll never be able to convict him. And if he's acquitted, even the *Khadis* won't be able to touch him."

I said: "If we try him under the Ethiopian Penal Code . . ."

One of the peculiarities of the law here, as set down by the Foreign Office in London, was that we operated with three separate and quite disparate penal codes—the Indian (which was more or less universal in the Colonial Territories), the British Military Code, and the local Ethiopian Code.

But Berren, who had been studying the rights and wrongs of this mish-mash, said: "Once the *Khadis* have come into it, we have to use the Indian Code, or else hand him back to them for trial. That's what it says in the book."

"And they set fire to his hands."

"Unless we stop them. We can, of course."

In a western police department, the problem would have been insuperable. Here, it was a great deal easier.

I said: "Tell the *Khadis* to investigate, and then hand him over to us when they've got a case."

"Yes, sir. What shall I do with him meanwhile?"

"Nothing you can do. Let him go."

"He'll cross the border, of course. His tribe's down in French Somaliland, over the frontier, most of them."

"Then it becomes their problem, doesn't it? Make out a report, send a copy to the *Khadis*, send a copy to the French in Djibouti, and then forget about it."

"Yes, sir."

But Issa Daoudi didn't go scot free. Two weeks later, the brother from Awash, who worked on the railway line, took the train down to Djibouti, searched him out, found him, and sliced his stomach open with a dagger.

And the feud, no doubt, even after all these years, is still going on. They last forever.

9

It always rankled abominably that we somehow had three sets of laws to contend with: the Indian, Military, and Ethiopian.

I was never able to find out just why these quite disparate codes were all in operation at the same time, but it was presumably something to do with the facts that:

1. Our occupation was neither military, nor civilian, but an odd mixture of both. London could never quite make up its mind which would be more "acceptable" to the Ethiopians—the overt use of military law, which would have implied conquest rather than a temporary holding mandate; or purely civilian law, which would have suggested a certain permanence.

2. The personnel of the occupying force was undoubtedly military in its entirety; one code for them and another for the people we governed would have seemed incorrect.

3. The Ethiopian Code had been thrown in as a quid pro quo during the extensive negotiations which, finally breaking down, led to the occupation of the Reserved Areas —a sop, of sorts, to suggest that we always knew our presence was only temporary.

Nonetheless, no system of law can work unless its provisions are clear-cut and not open to diverse interpretations, and I was quietly, and quite ineffectually, doing all I could to reduce these three systems to one—the Indian Penal Code, which is based on the normal Aristotelian concepts which are followed over most of the Western world today.

The Ethiopian Code was a token, and nothing more. Patently, we could make no use of it. In its physical property, the manual itself is pocketbook size, printed in English, and contains only eighty-four pages. In accordance with the Ethiopian's Hebraic origin, it is founded on the Law of Moses— or rather, on the Coptic Church's interpretation of it. It is overly simple, retributive, and demands an eye for an eye:

Article: "He who kills a man shall himself be killed in like manner. . . ."

Article: "He who cuts off the breast of a woman shall suffer ten years' imprisonment, except that if he cut off both breasts, the term shall be twenty years. . . ."

Article: "He who crushes the testicles of a man between two rocks, shall have his own testicles likewise crushed. . . ."

There were, of course, minor provisions which we could, and did on occasion, use—the relegation of ecclesiastical offenses to the various religious courts, for example; but this was desirable because of the peculiar ethnic demands of the people which could not always be satisfied by our own alien interpretations. As also in the rare cases of murder, we made full use of the Ethiopian proviso that permitted the payment of blood money by the criminal to the victim's family.

It was, therefore, the Military Code which offended me the

113

most. At my urging, the Governor had made repeated requests to London that it be repealed *in toto*. London would do nothing, not, I am sure, out of ill-will, but merely because of the tendency of civil servants the world over to pigeonhole anything that is not, in their own opinion, both desperately urgent and simple to achieve.

But, sometimes, that urgency can be injected into an argument, and I found the means to supply it on one of my trips, for inspection, down to Jig-Jigga.

And this time, I succeeded. It caused a fierce argument with the Governor, but it was worth it.

I have always thought that otiose protest is the most wasteful of human endeavors; and by the reverse token, nothing is more satisfying than a protest that pays off.

It all started with the trifling matter of an army rifle. I had returned from safari—and on safari you don't eat unless you hunt, and then you eat well—and I was chatting amicably with the Governor in his big, shady house, while Armina poured us coffee and kept interspersing comments in her charming kitchen Italian. My unloaded rifle was propped up in a corner of the veranda, and Sir Reginald remarked, quite mildly, that I was setting a bad example by hunting with a .303, which is illegal over most of Africa—merely to discourage the theft of army guns and ammunition. I pointed out that we practically made our own laws in this territory, that the Indian Penal Code said nothing about this, and neither did the Ethiopian Code; I was only contravening the military regulations which I'd long been trying to get repealed.

He became a little stuffy. He said: "That's all very well, but while the laws are in force, we will enforce them."

"And what are we doing to repeal them?"

He said, hurt: "I've written at least four times to London, as you well know."

"And they haven't answered you."

"No."

I said: "God dammit, Reggie, you're the Governor. They might at least have the courtesy to listen to you."

"Oh, I don't doubt they listen. Whether they want to take any notice of what I say, well . . . that's entirely another matter, isn't it?"

"Well, it shouldn't be. Parliament's been taken over by a bunch of idiots, and we ought to do something about it."

He looked at me a little suspiciously, and changed the subject. But the very hopelessness of our position vis-à-vis the distant authorities rankled too, and I was determined to take some sort of action. And shortly, an incident occurred that was just begging to become a cause célèbre.

On the outskirts of Jig-Jigga, the huge market town of the Ogaden, between the last whitewashed mud houses and the softly undulating green of the hills, there was an old, disused, dried-up well that the British army had dug when they were fighting the Italians here. And adjacent to it were the rusting remnants of an ancient pump. The well was no more than a deep hole in the ground into which grazing goats, and sometimes straying children, fell, and we were always going to have it filled in one day. And we were always going to get rid of the old pump too, perhaps by dropping it down the hole, because every time I walked this way I found it an eyesore and an intrusion on the gentle calm of the slopes, where zebra fed on the luscious grasses, and lion fed on the zebra. But the old hunk of machinery was heavy, and the weather was always hot, and so nothing was done about it; the broken pump stayed there, slowly rusting away under its coat of wind-blown sand.

One night, a rather stupid Somali policeman arrested a young Ethiopian for removing two rusted bolts from this lump of useless scrap iron; these bolts were handy for fashioning into arrowheads over a charcoal fire, and anyone could have helped himself during the daylight hours and nobody would have bothered him. But I suppose the darkness lent a felonious air to the incident, and Somalis were always looking for excuses to arrest Ethiopians—and vice versa—so, what with one thing and another, the young man was duly locked up for the night.

It was merely one of the trivial incidents that constituted our "crime," and the file was brought to me for routine signature. This was the Superintendent's job, really, but in the outlying stations they always liked to pay me these little courtesies when I visited them; it made me feel that I was really running the police force, which, to tell the truth, was very adequately run by the local people themselves.

When I saw what the offense was, I said: "Kick his arse and let him go, for God's sake."

The Superintendent was a young man named Hanson, an army Lieutenant from somewhere in the North of England, where they are not as sophisticated as we are in the South. He said hesitantly: "Well, I'm afraid he's been booked in already. The case will have to go to court now."

This too is part of the pattern. Someone signs a paper, fills in a form, and the mighty power of the Law moves on, relentless and inexorable; no one ever stops to think that the paper can be destroyed, and everything goes back to normal, or that trivia should not be permitted the luxury of compulsion.

It was a hot and humid morning.

I said wearily: "All right, what's he charged under?" I could imagine the petulance of the Magistrate when he learned that the stolen property consisted of two rusty bolts.

Hanson said: "Theft of government property, under the Indian Penal Code."

I said: "For God's sake, you realize you'll have to prove that it really is government property? If the army wrote off all their abandoned equipment when they left, if anyone even suggests that, the Magistrate is going to be after your blood. Hasn't he been at you once or twice already about preparing your cases properly?"

Hanson squirmed. "But everybody knows it's government property."

"What everybody knows is not necessarily acceptable in a court of law. If somebody once signed a bloody piece of paper writing the damned pump off, your whole case falls apart, he should never have been booked in the first place. For God's sake, two rusty bolts!"

"Well . . ." Hanson took time out to think, a thing he was not really very good at. He said brightly: "Then perhaps we could charge him under the Military Code. Interference with a military installation. Even if it's not government property any more, we can probably still insist that it's a military installation. I believe the Article is 205."

I was beginning to get angry with this eager young man. I said: "You know damn well I won't have anything to do with the Military Code. And under 205 he's liable to get a mandatory five years or something."

"Oh, surely not . . ." He found the thick brown book in the drawer of his desk and started leafing through the pages. He put it down at last and said: "Well, perhaps we should point out to the Magistrate that we don't really want to prosecute, but that once the man was arrested he had to be brought into court."

Hanson wasn't fooling anybody. I said: "All right, what's the penalty under 205?"

He was beginning to bluster. He said: "Well, 205 is part of the sabotage section, sabotage of military installations. No, we can't use that, can we?"

I said again: "What's the penalty?"

"Well, er, sabotage, under military law, is a capital offense."

"You mean, it's mandatory that we hang him if he's found guilty?"

"Er, yes, sir."

I said: "Well, that's nice. There are more ways than one to skin a cat, aren't there?"

"I beg your pardon?"

I said gently: "Charge him under the Military Code, Article 205."

Hanson stared at me. "We can't do that! A capital offense, it's mandatory!"

"So you said."

"But, but . . ."

I said again, talking to him slowly so that he'd understand: "You will prosecute under Article 205 of the Military Code, is that clear?"

"Yes, sir, but . . . but . . ."

I said: "Our job is to apply the law as it's written, not to question its wisdom. That's for the folks back home to do. If they don't like them, they should change them. Prosecute under 205."

I thought, *that'll teach them.*

Hanson said nervously: "Yes, sir."

It was an indication of trouble ahead. Hanson only called me sir when I was about to be fired.

*　　*　　*

The courtroom was a ramshackle, whitewashed building just off the Street of the Brothels, thatched with woven palm fronds and painted blue inside, to keep the flies away.

As always, there was a large crowd hanging around its doors, mostly Somalis, who are great litigators. Their long brown shanks were loin clothed with grubby rags or with goatskins, and the shadows of their ribs were clear on their hollow chests.

They were incredibly slim and beautiful, even elegant in their rags, their calm and heavy-lidded eyes showing no trace of the contempt they always felt for anyone who was not of their own tribe.

The crowd made way for me as I entered, the Ethiopians smiling affably, and the Somalis sniffing loudly; I took a seat on one of the wooden benches set there for the public.

Hanson was already there, prosecuting other cases when I arrived. He eyed me nervously. He was sweating, though it was early in the morning, and the perspiration was showing through his freshly starched bush jacket.

At a table on a raised dais at the end of the long room, the Magistrate was wiping his forehead delicately, his thin, classical features set in the kind of tolerant benevolence he affected for his erring children. He was one of the new school of civil servants sent out by the new Labour government, with a young and earnest attitude that was quite out of place in this happy-go-lucky land. His father was a Cabinet Minister in England's new government, and he was rather too big for his boots, a pedantic little fop whose name was Crest.

He looked up in surprise when I sat down, and nodded amiably, and then looked through his papers quickly to see what heinous offense had warranted my presence there, but could find nothing other than the day's regular crop of petty thefts, camel killings, and assault charges. Satisfied that there was no major case coming up, and that I was only there to keep an eye on the young prosecuting officer, he nodded to me once again, more convincingly, and then went on with the case he was trying, leaning forward earnestly to the accused, and nodding wisely as the court interpreter translated his weighty words.

Because of the huge number of languages and dialects spoken here, it had become our custom to carry on government matters either in English or Italian. The Danakil and the Galla, the Amharas and the Somalis, the Sidamo and the Shangalla could not understand each other unless they made use of a lingua franca. Once, that common tongue had been Swahili (a much-despised language) or Arabic (which almost nobody spoke anyhow); but today, after five years of Italian occupation, almost everybody, even in the remote bush, had at least a smattering of Italian. And so, our court translator worked in English and Italian, rather than the language of the accused; and everybody in court was happy.

Crest said to the interpreter: "Tell the accused I am disappointed to see him back in this court after my previous warning to him. I had thought better of him."

The interpreter said: "He says, 'your father was a camel, and your mother is a whore.' "

Crest nodded, and went on: "Tell him that if I see him here again within three months, I shall deal with him very severely."

The interpreter said: "He says, 'if you come back, they beat the hell out of you.' "

"Tell him that this time I shall be lenient because I think he has been led astray by his companions. Ten days' imprisonment."

He brought the gavel down sharply, and the interpreter said: "He says, 'you ought to be whipped, but he only give you ten days. You better tell your brother to send a cow round to the barracks.' " He caught my eye and said hastily: "Ten days."

The accused was bustled off to his first square meal in weeks, grinning happily at his good fortune, and shouting bright remarks to all his friends in court. They applauded him, vicariously delighted to share his luck.

Crest pulled his sticking bush jacket away from his chest, fanned himself with a file cover, and said: "Next case, Mr. Hanson."

Hanson looked at me, sighed, and took the plunge. He said:

"Case of Gabriel Dastata, an Ethiopian of Jig-Jigga, Article 205, Military Occupation Code."

The Magistrate frowned delicately, and took time out to throw me a frigid glance. He asked coldly: "Must we keep bringing up cases under the Military Code, Mr. Hanson? Isn't there something else he could have been charged under? I don't like applying military jurisprudence in a civil court."

Hanson said blandly, knowing that it was all or nothing now: "Yes, sir. There was a suggestion that he might be tried under the Indian Code, theft of government property, but there was difficulty in proving that the government still legally owned the property that was stolen, whereas it came from an installation that is incontestably military. We didn't wish to present an incomplete case, and if the court wishes . . . Er, it seemed wiser to change the charge."

"Quite, quite." The Magistrate sighed. He looked at his manicured nails and said to the orderly: "Bring me my Manual of Military Occupation Laws, will you? It's on the bookshelf in my office. And you might also bring me a glass of water. See if you can find some clean ice to put in it."

There was an Ethiopian lawyer in the courtroom, a man named Ato Desta, who (unofficially, of course) represented the Ethiopian interests. Technically, he was not only not allowed to be there; technically, we didn't even admit that he existed. It was one of those little niceties whereby, if he met the Governor on the street, each would studiously look the other way. His function was to keep Addis Ababa—*their* Addis Ababa—advised of what we were up to down in the Reserved Areas, and to remind us, gently, that they had no intention of giving up their claims to the area. I never felt, personally, that I had to go along with the pretense that he wasn't there, and we were on very amicable terms. For his part, he never tried to assert any kind of authority; a watching brief, he liked to call it. He was looking at me now with a perplexed look in his eye.

The orderly had gone off on his mission, and the Magistrate said to Hanson: "While we're waiting, Mr. Hanson . . . the stolen property is in the courtroom?"

"Yes, sir." Hanson held up two rusted bolts.

The Magistrate froze. He said at last: "And have you looked up the penalty for infringement of Article 205, Mr. Hanson?"

"Yes, sir."

"And what is . . .?"

Hanson said: "Hanging, sir."

It was the first time I ever saw Crest lose his considerable aplomb. He goggled. He swallowed hard and said: "Hanging?"

"Yes, sir." Hanson said firmly. "Mandatory."

I heard Counsellor Ato Desta choking, and saw him hurry from the court. The Magistrate's mouth was hanging open, and he closed it with a snap and looked at Hanson and then at me, and I thought for a moment that he was going to cry. Hanson was nonchalantly admiring the highly polished tips of his shoes.

The orderly came back with a glass of warm water and held it out to the Magistrate, saying: "No clean ice, sir."

Crest looked at me again, recovering at last, and I smiled as affably as I could at the little jerk. He gathered up his papers and said angrily: "This court is adjourned while I take this matter under advisement." He stepped down from the bench and left the room.

I hung around for a while, expecting him at least to send his orderly and ask to see me. But he didn't, and I decided he had quickly made up his mind to throw the case out and put in a report to the Governor.

One more little complaint would not have made much difference; but I was quite sure that Ato Desta, a tough and highly competent man, would now come into the argument, and just might supply that little touch of urgency that was needed.

There was an excited buzz of noisy conversation in the courtroom as translations were made into a dozen different languages. The prisoner stared at me with a puzzled look in his shrewd, intelligent eyes. I stared back at him for a moment, and then winked.

I drove back to Dire-Daua to accept whatever might be coming my way.

* * *

The Governor strode angrily up and down the long white room that was his office. He looked as though he ought to have been wearing riding boots and smacking them with a crop. There was hell to pay.

He kept saying: "How could you be so foolish, how *could* you?" I kept insisting that I merely applied the laws, not wrote them. He said: "You know how much I hate using that Military Code, you *know* that!"

"Yes, and so do I, Your Excellency."

He said: "And don't call me Your Excellency just because I'm angry with you. It was a monstrous thing to do. Monstrous." He said again: "How could you be so foolish? They'll probably insist that I fire you. If they don't fire me too."

"Or they might finally take those damn laws off the Statute Book."

"Yes, yes, yes, I know what you were up to, I'm not an idiot, you know. But . . ." He floundered with his hands in the air, and said: "This just isn't the way to do it! They'll fire *both* of us."

"I said: "I hardly think that's likely. All we've done . . ."

"All *you've* done . . ."

"All I've done is get Ethiopian backing for something that we all want. The Ethiopians will be as pleased as we will be when London, finally, repeals those laws. As they must, now."

He was very frigid indeed. He played his trump card and said, suddenly very cool and official: "You are presumably not aware that Ato Desta has sent off a cable to the Foreign Office in London. Not even through Addis Ababa, where it might have been killed! Direct to London! It's . . . unheard of! And we don't even know what the cable said."

"I know what it said. I have a copy of it."

The Governor said angrily: "Well, don't tell me, it was top secret and I'm not supposed to know what's in their secret cables." He looked at me suspiciously and said: "How did you get a copy?"

I shrugged: "Ato Desta is a friend of mine."

"Good God, we're not really supposed to know that he even exists!"

"And I went over to see him."

He stared at me. "You did what! Whatever for?"

"I wanted to be sure he understood what I was doing. I'm glad to say I had absolutely no explaining to do at all. He's not an idiot either."

Reggie sat down at last and held his head in his hands for a moment or two. He said: "What was in the cable?"

"In a rough paraphrase: 'We demand instant removal of Military Legislation still in abuse by the Occupation Authorities,' something to that effect, anyway. Exactly what we wanted."

The Governor groaned. "Abuse by the Occupation Authorities . . . Do you realize that a cable like that can result in a Royal Commission?"

I said: "We have nothing to hide from them. This is a damn good administration, and you and I both know that."

He groaned again. "A Royal Commission, in my Territory, an inquiry . . . Oh, my God!" He looked up and glared at me. "And what about Crest? He's furious!"

I said: "The hell with Crest. His job is to punish people

under the law, our job is to prosecute them under the law. The law is wrong, and now London knows it."

He said testily: "Yes, I know all about that." He sighed a long, sad sigh. "You'd better get that poor fellow out of jail, somehow or other."

"I did already."

"And how will the case be disposed of, now?"

I shrugged. "The policeman who arrested him made a stupid mistake. The prisoner is released."

"Released?" He got up and started pacing the office floor again, and said: "I suppose it's no good asking on whose authority?"

"On mine. We marked the file case dismissed and that's the end of it."

His eyes were like ice. "And suppose the Magistrate chooses *not* to dismiss the case?"

"Then he'll have to order him hanged. It's mandatory. Somehow, I can't see Crest doing that."

He made one last attempt: "The Ethiopians will sue us on his behalf."

"And you know damn well that that isn't true either. Ato Desta is a very bright man, he knows we've accomplished something that is going to make Addis Ababa very happy. It even reflects to his considerable personal advantage."

"The prisoner himself will sue us."

"No. I had him sent back to the bush with a bottle of *tej* in his pocket, a handful of brand-new bolts from the stores to turn into arrowheads, and a story he'll still be telling his children twenty years from now. And enjoying. They tell me he's as happy as a child in a sandbox."

"A Royal Commission, that's what will happen. I'm sure of it."

"Balls."

The Governor stopped his worrying and stared at me. I had

a feeling he didn't like me very much just now and was wondering where he could find a new Police Commissioner. But he was not a man to hold a grudge, and I knew that we'd be friends again tomorrow, and we were.

I left him sitting there, miserable and alone.

At the front door, I ran into Armina, and she looked at me sadly and said: "Why you always make my man so unhappy? He is a good man . . ."

I said: "I know that, Armina. And a good friend too, don't worry about it. Go and make him happy again, that's what you're here for. Take him to bed, make him happy."

"All right, I do that."

Her huge Somali eyes brightened suddenly, and she smiled and said: "I tell him you come for dinner again tomorrow, *va bene?*"

"*Va bene,* Armina. *Ciao.*"

I went back to my office and waited.

The Foreign Office acted with admirable dispatch, and in a few days' time the cables started coming in. There was no Royal Commission, and nobody was fired. They just told us to repeal the Military Occupation Laws in one fell swoop, all of them.

And in one fell swoop, that's what we did. All it needed was Sir Reginald's signature on another piece of paper.

10

Even though it was the British who, under mandate from the fledgling United Nations (of which Ethiopia was an original member), were administering huge areas of Ethiopian territory of which the Emperor insistently but patiently demanded the return, His Majesty Haile Selassie nonetheless held fast to his view that his Royal armies would best be trained by British officers on loan from England.

It was his view, rightly or wrongly, that the British were capable, reliable, and honest, and sufficiently free of political guile to guarantee a certain noninterference in his domestic affairs.

Certainly, in very broad general terms, the average Englishman is relatively free from the political deviousness of Machiavelli, Talleyrand, or Molotov. The French accusation of the *perfide Albion* arose, I am convinced, through his naïveté rather than his perfidy. He does, however, easily become intensely partisan, and he is easily seduced by those who earn his affection.

The officers training the Emperor's armies were no exception. They regarded our presence in the Reserved Areas as an insult to their own integrity and that of the Emperor himself; and they did not have his patience. They actively encouraged their troops to regard us as intolerable interlopers, along with those Ethiopians—our residents—who were on our side of the fence.

Most of them kept up the pretense that we weren't there; like a bastard in the family, they preferred not to talk about it. But on occasion, normal circumstance tended toward fracture of our uneasy peace, and then—then they would sit back and gleefully watch the results.

In the higher echelons, there was no real difficulty. But at the lower levels, the latent animosity sometimes came to the surface.

Dire-Daua itself was divided into two parts, into what, today, would be called the old city and the new. The new was composed of European-style houses, restaurants, cinemas, banks, and all the modern amenities with which the Italians, during their occupation, had surrounded themselves; it had been one of their major centers, and well developed as a flourishing cosmopolitan town. This is where all the Europeans of the area lived, the Greeks, Armenians, French, and even Italian traders and businessmen.

The old city lay just across a dry riverbed, a hundred yards or so wide, and consisted entirely of mud huts and *tukuls*, with a few stone churches and some mortar-built stores. As in the old city of Jerusalem or Jericho, its juxtaposition with its modern appendage is startling and fascinating. Here, in the Magallo, there were no roads, only winding dirt and stone tracks, while in Dire-Daua we had at least one good tarmac road. Here, there was no electricity nor piped water; on our own side of the track we had all these things, and a good deal more.

But the Magallo had a fascination all its own, and after that initial visit when I had ordered the barrier to remain open, I used to cross over quite frequently. I always went unarmed, not only because this was the correct thing to do (strict adherence to protocol demanded civilian clothes too, but with this I never bothered), but also because, while an unarmed man was in no great danger, there were plenty of people over there who would gladly cut a throat for the pleasure of acquiring a revolver or a rifle.

I would sit on a hard chair outside one of the cafés, watching the world go by and drinking beer or *tej;* and sometimes the known criminals from our side of the barrier who habitually took refuge there would come and stare at me, not jeering in any way but merely enjoying the fact that here I couldn't touch them. Any overt sign on their part that I was at a disadvantage here and could do nothing whatsoever toward their apprehension would have been far too crude a gesture; their inborn decency is quite remarkable. Sometimes, there would even be polite, and usually flippant, conversations between us:

"So this is where you've been hiding, Gabre."

"Yes, sir. I come back across the river, they going to put me in jail."

"Well? Is that so bad?"

"No women, sir, no tej. Is better I stay over this side." A beat, then: *"Maybe I come back one night to see my wife?"*

"If you do, we'll catch you."

"Yes, sir."

"Doesn't she know you're here? She can cross over to you easily enough."

"No, is better she stay over there, I got young girl over here, very young girl."

"Shall I tell her where she can find you?"

"No, sir, please, better you don't tell her nothing."

The Governor, of course, frowned on my visits there. When he heard, once, that I had been over there drinking with a notorious bandit who was wanted not only by our force but by the Emperor's men as well, he thought it might be time to complain.

I said, protesting: "I just want to see how the other half of the world lives. The Magallo's an interesting place, you ought to visit it yourself."

"You know I can't do that. And I wish you wouldn't. At least, not so often. One of these days we'll find your body thrown back over the barrier."

I didn't believe that, and I told him so.

He said: "Is it too early in the day for a Guinness?"

"No, I don't think so. What's on your mind?"

We were sitting in Windsor chairs, covered with bright green Somali shawls of the softest Kashmiri wool, in the living room of his big white house. Armina came in and poured us all some stout, in pewter mugs which she always kept cold in the icebox, then sat down with us.

He said: "All your wanted criminals hide out there, and that's why we've got so many unfinished cases on our files. They know they're safe once they cross that barrier."

"Of course. But when we hand the territories back, all that will be taken care of, won't it?"

"Yes, but meanwhile . . . when they see you over there, it's an indication of how powerless we really are. I don't like that."

"It also indicates our respect for proper behavior. At first, they wouldn't believe I'd sit there and not try to behave like a policeman, but when they found out that I respect their jurisdiction, it made them wonder if perhaps they should respect ours. And now, they do."

"Yes, that's true enough." He sipped his stout and said: "You haven't been here very long, have you? Not long enough to remember the fight we had? No, you weren't here then, that was in the South African heyday."

"I heard about it." My predecessor had described a fearful battle. The way he told it, only the Governor's insistence had prevented him from declaring personal war on Ethiopia. "But my information was probably not very good."

The Governor said: "The Ethiopian army was on maneuvers rather close by. A detachment camped in Magallo one night, and some of the men had a little too much to drink and decided they should teach us a lesson. And I'm afraid we learned afterward that their British officers had been activley encouraging them. I really can't think why they should do a thing like that, it was quite unforgivable. Anyway, they started firing across the border at us. The South Africans fired back, and in ten minutes there was a battle royal raging."

"And nobody was hurt."

"On our side, nobody. Over there, we don't know. Ato Waldo and I succeeded in getting a cease-fire before it went too far, but that meant that at least temporarily I had to recognize Ato's authority. It could have been extremely embarrassing."

Ato Waldo, an Ethiopian army officer, called himself the "Governor of Dire-Daua"; we called him Ato Waldo, and regarded him as just another citizen of independent means living on our side of the barrier, carefully pretending we knew nothing about his official capacity. It was all very farcical.

I said: "But you didn't bring this up for no reason at all, did you?"

"No, I didn't." He took a deep breath and said: "They're

holding maneuvers again, dangerously close to the border, just the other side of the hill."

Armina said: "Give rifles to all the Somalis, then there will be no more trouble from the Ethiopians."

He smiled at her benevolently and said: "No dear, we can't do that." He turned back to me with rather a twinkle in his eye. "Armina thinks this is part of Somali Ogaden."

I said: "Whether the Ogaden is Somali or not is a moot point, isn't it? Isn't that why we are here?"

He said quickly: "Yes, yes of course, you're absolutely right." There was a cold look in Armina's eyes, and I handed her my tankard for more beer. The Governor went on: "Anyway, don't go into the Magallo for the next few days. The Ethiopian army is much closer to us than I would have liked, but not close enough for a formal protest. Some of their detachments are certain to find their way into the Magallo some time or other, and we mustn't have another incident."

"And if there is one, what do you want me to do about it?"

He smiled happily, which he always did when he wasn't sure of something. "Well, we should cross that bridge if and when we come to it, don't you think? But meanwhile, the main danger is—good Heavens, supposing you were over there and got picked up by the army! It really doesn't bear thinking about . . ."

"All right, I'll keep clear for a few days, until they've gone on their way."

"Good. I'm sure you understand. I just want to make sure that everything stays quiet, and peaceful, and free from the kind of incidents we used to have here. It's really so much better now than it used to be."

I stayed with him for a while, thinking, as I so often did, what an extraordinarily kind and gentle man Sir Reginald was, quite unsuited to a difficult diplomatic post, and hating any and every need to assert his authority; but a thoroughly good man.

When I left him, he insisted that I take a case of Guinness along with me. He'd had some sent over from Hargeisa, and was anxious to share his good fortune with me.

*   *   *

Sure enough, three nights later, the shooting started.

I was in the outdoor restaurant-cinema again, dining off braised pigeon breasts with wild mushrooms and a vintage Pouilly Fouissé which had come up from Djibouti. I was watching, I remember, a film by Jacques Feyder, the 1935 classic *La Kermesse Héroique*, which concerns itself with one solution to military occupation—the welcoming and the seduction of the occupying forces by the local women.

The restaurant, Cloudot's, had become one of my favorite night spots, a long, semi-enclosed terrace well planted with trees and shrubs, with a big hibiscus-flowering garden in which a screen had been set up in view of the tables. The owner, Monsieur Cloudot, was a round and white-haired man who had a finger in all sorts of pies and who always insisted in the polite fiction that he bought his excellent wines from a nonexistent local wholesaler. In actual fact, he smuggled them up from the duty-free port of Djibouti, but we never chose to do anything about this because we happened not to have any laws covering smuggling; that was one of the things the diplomats in London had simply forgotten about.

The feature was nearly finished, and so was my dinner, when a policeman came in, found my table, and whispered that there was a little trouble outside.

Once on the street, I heard the shooting, and I hurried to my HQ. The Duty Officer was apprehensively calling in the patrols, who were taking their time about coming in, because they just couldn't understand why, if someone was shooting at them, they shouldn't shoot back; they were, after all, Ethiopians, and you can't open fire on an Ethiopian, whoever you are, without inviting trouble. But my orders on the subject had been firm. On the street outside the office people were gathering in little hushed groups; they thought the police building might be the safest place in case of real trouble. The Duty Officer was named Matheson, an Inspector. I asked him how long the firing had been going on.

"About fifteen minutes, sir."

"Any casualties?"

"Not so far."

"The patrols coming in?"

"Inspector Seyoum is rounding them up now."

I said: "Who's that firing down by the river? That sounds like our side of the fence."

"It must be patrol number four. Sergeant Aklilu and six *illaloes.*"

The *illaloes* were the supernumerary police, held in reserve in case of fire or riot. They were armed, but not very well disciplined, and not trained in the way our police were.

I said: "What the hell are the *illaloes* getting in the act for?"

"Apparently a few shots went through the windows of their barracks, but Seyoum will get them out of there."

"If I know Seyoum, he's giving them all the encouragement he thinks he can get away with."

Matheson said: "I don't think so, sir. He's a very responsible sort of fellow."

"You don't know his sense of humor. Take a truck and bring those bloody *illaloes* in."

"Yes, sir."

He went off, and I found Inspector Gabre, who was the most intelligent officer, British or Ethiopian, in the whole police force. He spoke English, French, Italian, and German with no trace of an accent. A mild-mannered, scholarly sort of man with an easy, comfortable manner.

I said: "I thought we might go over there and talk them into a cease-fire, what do you think?"

He smiled. "Since none of our men is allowed to fire back, I think that might be the best thing to do."

"Will they cut my throat?"

"No, sir, I don't really think they'll do that."

"What about yours?"

He laughed. "Less improbable, perhaps, but after all, it's the Royal Ethiopian Army, not just bandits."

"All right, we'll leave our guns behind."

"Yes, I think that would be best."

There was a strange, distant rumbling noise in the air that sounded like the very distant fire of heavy artillery, and Gabre said: "I think we'd better hurry."

The barrier was still open, but the sentry there had been reinforced by four men; they were lying down in the sand, facing Magallo, their rifles ready, and a small knot of townsfolk had gathered on the opposite bank, wondering whether they should try to make the crossing or not in the face of the menacing rifles.

I said to them: "None of you fires his rifle, under any circumstances. If anyone tries to cross, let them through. If they're armed, disarm them first."

Gabre called out to the people on the other bank, and an aquaintance hurried over, one of our own professional thieves. He carefully remained on the other side of the barrier, but doffed his white toupee in a courteous gesture. A few other old friends gathered round, and I shook hands with some of them, and Gabre spoke to them in Amharic and found out that there were eighty or ninety soldiers in the town, most of them drunk.

The noise of the distant thunder was approaching fast, and then someone shouted, and Gabre said: "The *tug*, quickly!" He grabbed me by the arm and we fled.

The *tug* is a wall of water that once in a while pours down any dry riverbed in these parts, and this was a big one. There was no sign of rain anywhere within sight, but perhaps as much as a hundred miles away there would have been a cloudburst in the mountains. Now the great wall of water, five feet high, was racing toward us down the riverbed, roaring like thunder in its fury. It was the first time I'd seen it. Gabre dropped my arm and picked up a screaming child as we hurried to the opposite bank in ankle-deep sand and scrambled up it.

And then, the *tug* hit.

It went by us with a terrible roar, the white water churning over and over, with bits of timber, and roots, and boxes, and bundles of thatch, and parts of whitewashed mud buildings all mixed up with it. I saw a group of three dead goats, tethered together, rolling over and over, and there were a lot of chickens too. A tall pole stood on end for a moment, either a palm tree or perhaps a field telephone post, and then crashed down into the water and disappeared. In the darkness, with only the eerie light of the white moon, bright enough to read a paper by, it was a startling and rather splendid sight. Crowds were running to the banks, watching it, and the shooting had stopped, though it started again in a few moments, three or four hundred feet to one side of us. I could hear the whine of bullets, but nobody else seemed concerned, so I didn't let it bother me.

We pushed our way through the crowd, and Gabre sent two small boys running off for information. In a short while, they came running back, and Gabre smiled and said: "In Toka's café, I think you know it."

We walked through a little square, almost deserted now, with broken rubble all around our feet, with goats and chickens and an occasional cow wandering, and found two Ethiopian army officers sitting under the bright flare of a kerosene lamp at the café's door. They stood up as we approached, and shook hands and bowed several times, and I greeted them in Italian and French and English, and said: *"Te'ena ysterling."* But neither of them spoke anything but their own language, so it was all in Gabre's capable hands. I gave the café owner, Toka, a couple of silver Maria Theresa dollars and told him to keep the glasses filled. They were the thick, heavy glasses, cut from beer bottles.

I said to Gabre: "It's all in your hands, you know what to do. If any of their British officers turn up, leave it all to me. But otherwise . . . you handle it. Tell them we've already instructed our men not to fire, and take it from there."

My own presence was a symbol, nothing else, and I was well aware of Gabre's capability. But first, he explained gently, we would have to indulge the little courtesies, to pass the time of day; it would be impolite to come to the point too quickly.

He translated for me as we asked after each other's health, and the health of our respective families; we discussed horses for a while, and food, and women, and the coming wedding of the Duke of Harar who, I pointed out, was a personal friend of mine.

One of the Ethiopian officers was a Major, the other a Lieutenant. The Major was a rather stolid man of the old school, a peasant who looked out of place in his uniform. He asked, through Gabre, if I didn't know that I was not supposed to be in the Magallo? He wasn't unpleasant about it, just searching for information. I told him that his men were not supposed to be firing into Dire-Daua either, and he agreed, after a little thought, that this was so. He told me that he'd been here during the last conflict and that two of his men had been wounded by our fire; I hoped they weren't hurt badly, and he shrugged and said: "Soldiers, it is what we all expect." The firing was still going on, and I began to wonder how long they'd keep it up. I assumed that the civilians on our side of the border had sense enough to take shelter, though stray bullets can kill just as easily as aimed ones.

But at last I realized that Gabre and the Major were arguing about the battle and were coming to some sort of agreement. The Lieutenant, on the order of his superior officer, got up and bowed to me, and went out; he was young and well groomed, a city man.

Gabre turned to me and said: "The troops will be withdrawing now." He smiled and said: "The Major has pointed out that no one has been firing into the town, it's just that they are firing their rifles into the air in their exuberance. He's quite distressed that we thought they were firing at us."

"Of course. I hope you told him we understand that."

"Yes, I did. I said nothing about the shots that went through the barracks, a question of his dignity, you understand."

"Let's pretend that didn't happen either. And let's all have some more beer."

Toka was bringing it, a fat, dirty man with a bulging belly, when a British army officer came in, one of the advisers.

He was a thin, sandy man with a small moustache, quite young and eager and not very agreeable, although I was surprised to see that he spoke quite fluent Amharic, a language that I'd still not been able to learn—surely the most difficult language in the world—although six or seven other languages at the tip of my tongue had made languages reslatively easy for me to learn.

He was indignant at finding me there when he discovered who I was, but I pulled rank on him and told him to shut up and have a drink, and when he protested that he didn't recognize "our" presence, I said: "I don't give a damn who pays you or who pays me, you're still in the British army and you'll bloody well do as you're told, or I'll drag you back to my side of the fence and have you court-martialed. I never heard such insubordination."

He sat down, reluctantly, and when I told him I'd come to put an end to the war, he fiddled with his moustache and said gloomily that you couldn't always control the troops when they got a drop of *tej* inside them, but he'd see what he could do. Gabre smiled and said nothing, and then the shooting stopped abruptly and the young Englishman got up and said: "Well, I'll go and see if I can call them off, but I won't promise anything." He glowered at me and said: "After all, they don't approve of your being here."

I thought it would be discourteous to tell him that a junior Ethiopian Lieutenant was already implementing an armistice, so I said nothing.

He went out, and Gabre explained to the Major that some-one else was going to stop the war too. The Major threw back his head and roared with laughter, and clapped me on the back and said: "Good, good," the only English word he knew. Then Gabre smilingly excused himself, remembering, like the good executive officer he was, that we had no patrols out and that they ought to be put back to work.

He said: "Will you come too?"

But the Major was insisting on buying the next round. I said: "No, I'll wait for a while."

"Shall I send a car for you when the river goes down again?"

It would take three or four hours for the water to go, and meanwhle Gabre would have to struggle through thigh-deep mud.

I said: "No, I'll walk back. Let me know if you need me over there."

"Yes, of course."

Everybody stood up and shook hands with everybody else, and bowed and smiled and made polite little comments, and when Gabre had gone, the Major and I settled down to drink and to talk about our various conquests. Toka came to the table and plumped himself down and translated from Amharic into Italian, and a crowd gathered at the door, knowing that the armistice parley had been a success; they were very impressed at being in on a summit meeting of this kind.

139

We made fulsome and exaggerated compliments about each other's country, and we drank a great deal of beer and ate some cheese, and the Major promised to send me some coffee from his farm and some *beri-beri* which, apart from being the name of a disease, is also a very potent kind of pepper, compared with which red-hot chili tastes like chalk. He told me where there was a family of wild boar just ripe for the pot, and I told him about the spoor of a really big leopard I had seen down by the entrance to the Madar Pass. We almost got a hunt together there and then, but we remembered we were both on duty and so we had some more beer instead.

It was getting light by now, and Toka fell asleep at the table, and a small boy turned out the kerosene flare, so the Major and I got up, rather heavily, and walked over to the riverbed and stood there trying to talk for a while, neither of us much succeeding in understanding the other's language but knowing that we were friends, and then I struggled across through the mud, noticing all the sadness that was in the broken fragment of a small house that had been lodged in the middle of the river, its thatch torn away, the red mud of the walls still bonded together with the wattle poles and coconut fiber; someone had once lived there and was now, perhaps, searching downstream for the pathetic pots and pans and pieces of furniture, and perhaps children too, that the little house had once contained.

The *tug* struck two or three times a year, and they still went on building their huts close by the banks where they would be torn away.

The Major made a little speech, in Amharic, and I made another, in English, and though neither of us knew what the other was saying, each of us also knew that it was the gesture that mattered. We shook hands, and he turned on his heel and went back among the mud huts, a barrel-shaped man with the gait of a farmer, and I struggled back through the knee-deep mud to the peace and the quiet of the little European enclave.

The patrols were on the streets again, and I looked at the reports which were just starting to come in.

One man had been hurt in the shooting, one of the *illaloes*, but it was only a flesh wound and not very serious; and now, every decent citizen was in his bed. The early morning was cool and peaceful, and the waiters in the cafés had already come to work and were washing down the night's accumulation of dust and dirt, and there was the smell of the strong Harar coffee in the air.

I found Matheson half asleep at his desk, and told him to get a detail of prisoners sent down to the riverbed to help clear away the debris and get the drowned animals disposed of before they began to rot in the heat of the day. The Ethiopian clerk said: "Someone will eat them, sir . . . they will not rot." There was plenty of food in the Magallo, but there were poor people there too, to whom fresh meat from upstream would be a welcome blessing.

The barbed-wire fence, of course, remained unhappily in position where it had always been, though its gate was now left permanently open. On the day that came at last when we went away, I was happy to see a party of Ethiopians tearing it down and hurling it out of the way. But for the time being it remained as a constant reminder that the powers above us, in a cold and draughty London office, far from the hot sun and the open plains, were determined that these people should remain separate from us, should put up with the fancy that their country was not really their own.

I went over to the Governor's house and found him waiting for me on the veranda, wearing pajamas and a dressing gown. He said: "Well, is it all over?"

"Yes. One man hurt, but not badly."

"You didn't find it necessary to go over there, did you?"

"No, sir."

He knew I was lying. He smiled and said: "Good. We really

141

mustn't put ourselves in the position of having to negotiate with them, must we?"

I went back to my house, and Gabre was there, standing by the big iron gate and stroking my cheetah, Satan.

He said: "Bad news, I'm afraid. During all that shooting, someone broke into the bank."

"Oh my God. What did they get?"

"Twelve bags of Maria Theresa dollars, and about three thousand pounds in English currency. We won't know exactly till the morning, they're making a tally now."

"Who's working on it?"

"Inspector Berren. We think they were Somalis."

"Any reason for thinking that? Or just your natural chauvinism?"

He smiled. "Oh no, we have our quota of thieves too. But a girl saw four or five Somalis, the Issa Mahmoud tribe she thinks, near the bank's back door, just standing there and looking suspicious. One of them threatened to beat her if she didn't move off."

"All right, have Berren report to me at ten o'clock."

"Yes, sir."

"I'll be in the office at nine. Good-night, Gabre."

"Good-night."

Satan was in a bad mood that night; he ran his claws savagely down my calf when I disturbed him by turning over in my sleep.

And in the morning, I took a look at the affair of the bank robbery; it was our first, and our last, and we never solved it.

11

The bank was not a commercial building in the ordinary sense of the word; it was merely an old store that stood discreetly behind one of the smaller hotels, a matter of five hundred yards from the railway station. It was built mostly of stone and concrete, and when the bank had taken it over, a few years ago, its Greek manager had installed an iron grill over the big front door; the back, however, which gave onto a rather untidy alleyway, was more or less as it always had been, its lightweight door having been replaced with a much heavier one.

It was this door that had been broken open. Inside, a second door of soft-iron bars had been dealt with efficiently (it was not much of an obstruction) by being bent out of shape with a pole of ironwood.

The safe, which contained a great deal of money, had not

been touched, presumably being too strong for the amateurs who had broken in, and they had merely taken what turned out to be two thousand three hundred and fifty pounds in English currency, that somehow had been left lying around, and twelve heavy bags of a thousand Maria Theresas each, which had been brought in by various traders during the day and were stored in a corner under a counter awaiting their individual counts.

And a Singer sewing machine, which was used for making up currency bags, had been stolen from its table just inside the main entrance. (Throughout the whole of Africa, you will find these machines in great abundance; every little village has at least one or two treadle models.)

Berren had a full report for me when I arrived, and the girl who had seen the robbers was there too, a heavyweight, dull-witted Amhara in a bright dress of a highly flowered cotton print; she had two tiny burn marks on her forehead, one at each temple, which signified she had once been a slave.

She was not much help. She said that the Somali whom she had mostly clearly seen "looked like all Somalis, they all look alike" and that he had been armed with a spear which he had shaken at her in a threatening manner. She had seen three other men, but not very clearly, and one of them had been carrying a long pole of mangrove wood—the beam they had used for twisting the iron bars out of shape to permit their passage.

We learned that two of the Sabena trucks had been parked overnight in the alleyway, with their drivers supposedly asleep on board, but when we brought them in for questioning we learned that they had both spent the night in a brothel two blocks away. There had, apparently, been no other witnesses.

The Greek manager did not seem too upset about his loss. He was a sharp, shrewd man named Demetrios who spent most of his time playing poker and slowly acquiring a fortune as a result. (There was a rumor that he had once put up his bank against the rundown Splendid Hotel, and had won the hotel with a pair of tens.)

I said: "Do you usually leave bags of currency lying around like that?"

He shook his head. "No. It's just that we couldn't find the key to the storeroom where we would normally have left them overnight."

"And there'd be, no doubt, a great number of Somalis coming and going through the late part of the afternoon?"

He shrugged: "Oh yes, quite a fair number. There was a camel market going on down the line today, they were bringing the proceeds in."

"Would you recognize Issa Mahmoud Somalis as belonging to that particular tribe?"

"No, of course not. Who could?"

The Governor would have spotted them at once; a way of wrapping their loincloths around them, the decoration on a beaded pouch one of them might have been carrying . . . But there weren't many experts of his caliber around.

I said: "They'd almost certainly need some sort of transportation. That's a lot of weight to carry."

"A truck? I hear there were two Sabena trucks there overnight."

"Yes, there were. But the drivers weren't there, and the trucks were not moved. Sabena has a daily speedometer check, the night and morning readings were the same, just as they were supposed to be."

"Camels then."

"Or a mule, yes. One of them, at least, was carrying a spear. That presupposes they'd come in from the bush."

"Perhaps. But not necessarily so."

"One of the sergeants is out there now, trying to find out if anyone living close by heard a truck during the night. We know, more or less, when it must have happened. There was a patrol passed by at ten minutes past eleven, and one of the *illaloes* first reported seeing the broken door at fifteen minutes past two, though he's not too sure of the time. There's not much traffic around at that time of night, and a truck might have been stopped for a routine check. But a heavily loaded camel—no one would bother about it."

"The alleyway should show tracks, it's only a dirt road."

"Camel spoor all over. A mule was there too, and a lot of footmarks, bare feet and sandals. Doesn't mean very much."

He sighed and stood up. "Do you expect to catch them?"

"Probably not. We'll try."

"Good. I've got insurance, of course, but it's in Athens, it'll be years before I'm reimbursed."

When he had gone, Gabre told me he was making inquiries among the known thieves, and that he had put one of the Somali sergeants onto the case, a Yebir tribesman named Wabro. The Yebir are a subdivision of the Mitgan, and their hatred of the Issa Mahmoud is quite remarkable.

He said: "If they really were Issa Mahmoud, then Sergeant Wabro will find them."

"You believe that?"

He grimaced. "We're looking mostly for a sewing machine, a Singer. They'll sell that to the first buyer they run into."

He was right.

We found the sewing machine two days later. A Somali of the Issa Mahmoud tribe had sold it to a Galla woman who lived on the edge of the river that separated us from the Magallo; she had paid him two goatskins for it. We found the pole they had used on the evening of the same day, pushed in among a pile of other poles that were to be used for building; the marks of the iron bars were still quite clearly visible on it. And we found part of the currency blowing out in the desert beyond the barracks of the King's African Rifles; it was a fair assumption that the robbers had simply thrown it away, since so much

English currency in the hands of Somalis would have aroused a great deal of suspicion, though it's also possible that they didn't know what kind of money it was and wanted to take no chances finding out.

But the bags of silver dollars—that was another story altogether. The Maria Theresa is very common currency, acceptable everywhere (where paper money is not), and cannot possibly be traced. These coins, incidentally, are still being minted today, in Austria, and sent to Ethiopia; and they are still stamped "1842"—the date of the original minting.

It was a week later that the break came, and it came from an unexpected source—Sir Reginald's Italian driver.

He was a heavily built, red-haired mechanic from Northern Italy, an introspective sort of man with very pale blue eyes that always seemed blandly distracted, as though he were permanently daydreaming. Officially, he was a civilian, and attached to the police force as a kind of adviser. He ran the workshops, and kept all our various vehicles in order, with the help of the Ethiopian staff he was training.

His name was Lucertola, a strange name; it means *lizard*. He was a first-rate mechanic, a marvelously competent, though reckless, driver, and he was not much liked by anybody in Dire-Daua except the Italian civilian drivers whom he helped considerably from time to time in the matter of spare parts for their vehicles; our stores were in a permanent state of imbalance as a result of his friendships. I was never able to find out just what it was that made the Ethiopians and the Somalis distrust him so much. With me he was always correct, affable, and a trifle sly; I rather liked him.

I was watching him put a rebuilt gas pump into my Lancia in the police garage one day, when he threw down his wrench with a clatter, wiped at the sweat on his neck, and said, grinning: "*Commandante*, would you like to know where all those Maria Theresa dollars are?"

I was startled. Lucertola kept very much to himself, and though very talkative, he seldom actually said anything. I couldn't really believe that he had any inside information.

I said: "Well, if you know where they are, you'd better tell me."

"Isshak knows all about it."

"Isshak?"

"Quel domestico del governatore."

Isshak was Sir Reginald's cook, a young Somali who had been with him for five or six years, and Lucertola grinned and said: "He's an Issa Mahmoud, and he knows all about it."

"Have you told this to anybody else?"

"No, sir."

"You'd better have a word with Sergeant Wabro."

"Wabro? He won't believe a word I say, and then he'll tell all his Somali friends. And one night, they'll cut my throat."

"All right, leave it to me. But you must have some reason for believing that?"

He shrugged. "One of my friends at Sabena, his Somali loaders were talking about it."

"Issa Mahmouds?"

"Yes, most of them."

"Anybody outside the tribe know about it?"

He shook his head. "If they did, they'd inform on them at once, a chance to get back on some of their old enemies."

"All right, I'll talk to Wabro about it."

But I didn't. Instead, I went round to see Armina. Sir Reginald was lunching with the Railway Administration, and their lunches usually lasted most of the afternoon, so I expected to find her alone. But her sister was with her, a much younger girl whom I had never met before; she had just come up on a visit from Mogadiscio, and Armina, delighted, made the introductions.

"This is my sister, her name is Josephine."

I said: "I have a cheetah named Josephine."

She was not only much younger than Armina, she was also a great deal better looking. She was tall, and very straight, with a rather plump, cheerful face, and the more I looked at her the more attractive she seemed to be. She still had the incredible feline grace of the young Somali women, extremely callipygian, with graceful flowing movements to her limbs.

It's an odd thing about the Somali women. When they bend down, as they do to wash clothes in the river, for example, they normally keep the legs stiff, so that the whole of the torso seems to be detached, seems to be an entity of its own. The Arabs, the Amhara, the Danakil, all the others crouch to do their ground-level chores. Not so the Somalis; they stand, and bend down, and in the course of time it gives them very finely developed buttocks and an articulation at the waist that is quite remarkable. Unhappily, they soon lose it; they age very early, and then they tend to run to fat, even in the bush where their food is quite limited.

Her breasts were still good, very high and firm, and not flopping around as her sister's did. Her skin was flawless, honey colored, and her hair was unusually fine, set in a very modern style; Mogadiscio, capital of Italian Somaliland, was also a very cosmopolitan town.

I said to her: "What do you do in Mogadiscio?"

She laughed. "Do? I don't work, if that's what you mean. I have friends, lots of friends, they take care of me."

Her Italian was easy and fluent, much better than Armina's. It appeared that the two of them had gone on very disparate ways—Armina with Sir Reginald to his very remote bush-country home, and Josephine to the sophisticated luxury of the city.

I said: "And are you really sisters?"

"The same mother, different fathers."

"But you're both Issa Mahmoud?"

Her laughter was very contagious. "Issa Mahmoud? Yes, I suppose we both were, once. Now . . ." she shrugged, "we're not tribal any more, that's only in the desert."

"There are a lot of Issa Mahmouds in the towns too. In Mogadiscio, in Dire-Daua."

She nodded. "Of course. Everywhere."

"Some of them broke into our local bank the other night, did you hear about that?"

"Yes, I heard. Armina told me."

I was not looking at Armina. But I was acutely, very acutely, conscious that she had almost frozen. It was as though she knew, at once, what I had come for. I turned to look at her, and her eyes were very bland and distant, almost glazed. I was astonished (and aware that I had no reason to be) at the bright intelligence there, as though she had read my mind very thoroughly and had leaped on a dozen steps ahead of me.

It wasn't exactly fear; it was more of a momentary panic, very well controlled, or even a sudden suspicion. And I had a very strong feeling that if Isshak knew about the robbery, then she did too. I had no reason whatsoever for this assumption, but her sudden access of guilt was very clear. I found it alarming.

Josephine was laughing again, a bright, delighted laugh of genuine amusement. She said: "If they really were Issa Mahmouds, you'll never catch them. They are the best at everything, even thievery."

Armina excused herself to go and order coffee, and as she turned back to look at me I said: "And do you think I could have a word with Isshak?"

She was very prompt, very cool, all smiles again: "Isshak? No, you can't. He's at the market. Why don't you come round this evening and talk to him?"

"All right, it's not urgent."

"Or I can talk to him for you. Shall I do that? If you tell me what it's about?"

"Don't worry, I can wait."

We chatted for an hour or so, the three of us, and Josephine showed me the Kashmiri shawls she'd brought up with her from Mogadiscio, and we drank coffee and then beer, and no one said anything more about these missing Maria Theresas. But by the time I left, I was quite certain that Armina knew all about the robbery, that she was terrified that I might say something untoward about it to the Governor, and that sooner or later she'd want to find out from me exactly how much I knew—if anything.

And on the way home from work that evening, I met her wandering down the road with Isshak, the cook. They'd been out buying cheeses together, she told me, and was surprised and delighted that we'd met so fortuitously.

It was all a little transparent.

She said brightly:"You wanted to speak to Isshak. Well, here he is now."

I said: "No, it doesn't matter any more."

"I won't listen, go on, talk to him."

"No, no, it's all finished now."

She persisted: "It was about the bank robbery, wasn't it?"

"What makes you think that?"

"Well, he's an Issa Mahmoud, so you think he must know something about it. But just because one Issa is a thief, it doesn't mean to say that all the others are, does it?"

"No, of course not."

"Well, then?"

He stood there, the young cook, looking sullen and highly suspicious of me.

She went on: "There are dozens of Issa Mahmouds in town, you said so yourself."

"Yes, I know that."

I was lost, and I knew it. I said gently: "I just wanted to talk to one of their tribesmen, any one of them who might be on the administration staff, to see if he could find out anything for me."

She shrugged. "What could he do? He is a simple man, a peasant, he doesn't know anything."

"No, I suppose not. It was just an idea."

She pushed it too hard, and said: "Besides, you should ask Reggie first, wouldn't that be more polite? It's rude, no?, to talk to his servant without asking him first? *Ne' vero?* Isn't that true?"

I was very angry with her. I said: "All right, let's go round right now and ask his permission. Right now." I took her by the arm, quite gently, but she held firm and looked at me straight in the eyes and said: "Why do you want to hurt him always? He is your friend, you *know* he's your friend."

"I don't want to hurt him, I just want to ask if I may interrogate his cook, for God's sake!"

"Isshak knows nothing. Nothing at all, I promise you. If he knows, I know too, it's very simple, and he knows *nothing.*" She was becoming agitated, and her Italian, never very good, was getting a bit ragged. But hardly stopping for breath, she said: "Have you had your dinner?"

"No, of course not." I thought she was going to invite me over to Sir Reginald's.

She said, smiling again now: "Then why don't you take Josephine out for dinner? She's bored in the house, and she likes you, she likes you a lot."

I had already long decided that if the Governor's mistress were indeed mixed up in this robbery, there was absolutely nothing I could do about it. I had decided that all I could do was back off, add a little more pretense to the pretense of our existence there. The slightest suspicion of such unpleasantness would have broken his heart, and you don't have to be a policeman all the time, particularly when you are an amateur. Rightly or wrongly, I felt that I could not even broach the matter to him.

I said, knowing I'd been thoroughly defeated: "All right, why don't you ask her to meet me at Cloudot's?"

She was bright and friendly again, absolutely sure of herself, arriving at the right conclusion for the wrong reasons. She said: "No, no . . . Come round now and invite her yourself, *va bene?*"

"*Va bene.*"

Sir Reginald was there with Josephine when we got to the house, and he poured me a drink happily, and when I told him I was taking Armina's sister to dinner, he looked pleased, but said: "Well, I think she's going out tonight with George Addison, from the railway. He's calling for her later on."

Addison was the head of railway administration, a very hearty sort of man from the North country in England, a lady-killer who could never resist the charms of so splendid a visitor as Josephine. He was a good railway man, but rather boisterous and loud-spoken.

But Armina was speaking rapidly and earnestly to Sir Reginald, and he was smiling at her benignly and trying to get a word in once in a while, looking at me from time to time as though there was some hidden joke between them.

He turned to me at last and said, almost whispering: "Armina says that Josephine really wants to go out with you, she doesn't like George very much, so you'd be doing all of us a favor. And now I'll have to tell Addison that she's got a headache, won't I? I'm not very good at that sort of thing."

I said: "I'm sure Armina will come to your rescue, Reggie."

"Yes. Yes, I hope she will."

We dined together at Cloudot's later that evening, and, of course, Addison's number-two man, Harry Blake, was sitting at the next table eyeing us throughout the whole of the dinner.

I found Josephine to be a very entertaining companion, bright, witty, and full of all the scandal from over the border.

That, I remember, was a Wednesday.

On the following Friday, Sergeant Wabro came in to report. He gave me the names of two of the robbers, and said he was unable to find out who the other two were. He told me that they were all from Ferfer, the border town between Italian Somalia and the Ogaden, and that they had now crossed over the border out of our territory.

I said: "What about the bags of silver dollars?"

He was stolid, impassive, and perhaps a little ashamed that his thieves had kept one jump ahead of him. He said: "My information is that the bags were all put in a big wooden box and hidden here, somewhere in town, until last Wednesday night."

"And then?"

"Then they were put on board a Sabena truck and taken to Ferfer, and then off-loaded in the desert somewhere, where they were picked up by camels."

"Where was the hiding place in Dire-Daua?"

He shook his head: "I don't know, sir." He fidgeted for a moment, and said at last: *"C'e una persona* . . . there's somebody in His Excellency's house who knows where it was hidden."

Una persona; it could be a man or a woman.

I said: "Do you know who that is?"

"My informant says it's Isshak, the cook."

"Anybody else?"

"No, sir." I still don't know whether he knew or not.

"All right. How good is your information?"

He shrugged. "Isshak's wife told my informant. Either one of them might have been lying."

"Then you'd better leave it to me."

"Yes, sir."

I sent for Lucertola, and when he came in, I said: "According to Wabro, the money seems to have left town now. So where was it being hidden? You do know, don't you?"

He was not in the least embarrassed. He said blandly: *"Commandante, non so niente. I know nothing.* Only . . . over at Sabena they say it was in the storeroom of the Governor's house." He shrugged. "Maybe it's true, maybe not, you can never tell when a Somali is telling the truth. Usually they're lying. But they say it was in the stone storeroom where he keeps the Djibouti demijohns." He shrugged again. "The Governor never goes there himself, he wouldn't know about that."

"Who keeps the key to it?"

"Isshak."

"And you really believe that Isshak was the brain behind it all?"

"No, signore."

"So? Who was it?"

He hesitated for a long time. He said at last, very carefully: "The loaders over there, the Somalis—they say it was *quella vaccha. That cow."* . . . His pale blue eyes were bland and innocent.

I said: "And why did you choose not to tell me about this?"

His astonishment was almost comic opera, the sacristan finding Cavaradossi's breakfast basket empty. He spread his arms wide in an expression of indignation: "But I only just found out!"

"And you never saw fit to drop even a hint to His Excellency? That's surprising. He's always been very, very good to you."

He nodded. The astonishment was quite gone. He said gravely: "Yes, sir, of course. And that's why I never mentioned it."

Poor Demetrios never did get his insurance. There'd been some technical error in making out the coverage, so he finally, three months later, wrote off twelve thousand silver Maria Theresa dollars, two thousand three hundred and fifty English pounds, and one Singer sewing machine, which we never bothered to retrieve from the poor Galla woman who had paid, in perfect good faith, two good goatskins for it.

And on the following Monday, Isshak simply disappeared. The scuttlebutt in the police barracks, reported to me by Inspector Seyoum, was that Sergeant Wabro had threatened to slice him open with his dagger unless he left town. Wabro stolidly denied it, but, as Lucertola had said, you never could tell when a Somali was telling the truth.

12

The long-awaited wedding of the Duke of Harar came at last, and the Governor and I were invited to the palace for the reception which was to be given afterward.

I had never seen the Duke looking so glum. Even the arrival of a brand new motor for his beloved Lancia, brought from Italy by the Sabena Trucking Company and smuggled through Djibouti, Ethiopia proper, and into our own Reserved Areas, could not console him.

We sat together in Cloudot's on the evening before the ceremony, his last night—for a while at least—with his lovely mistress Maria.

Harar itself is one of the most fascinating towns in Africa, a center of immense historic importance, but to a resident of the Duke's sophistication, it was backward and even barbaric.

It lacked the "European" amenities of Dire-Daua, and two or three times a week he would race down the winding road from his capital and spend the evening drinking, chatting, or playing poker with his friends, in Cloudot's cheerful little restaurant.

It was an escape, for him, from an era and a place that were essentially African, into a relatively modern and cosmopolitan world—the exchange of culture for civilization.

He loved Harar, the birthplace of his father, the Emperor; but he was out of kilter, perhaps, with its place in history.

Until 1887, when Harar was conquered and annexed by the great King Menelik II, founder of modern Ethiopia, it had been a Moslem state. (It was at this time that Ogaden, a little farther to the east, was also annexed; hence the Ethiopian claim to that territory and our own subsequent presence there.) Its pagan Galla tribes, who had once occupied more than a third of Ethiopia's territory, had been forcibly converted to Islam, and in the sixteenth century it had been entirely surrounded by a massive stone wall, which stands to this day, built by a Lieutenant of the Immam Ahmed el Ghazi, known to the Ethiopians as the Gran, or Left-handed Man, a military leader whose name figures extensively in Ethiopia's constant wars against the Moslems on their Eastern borders.

Its narrow, dirt-surfaced streets are flanked by open-fronted stores, and the crush of its people, of its donkeys, chicken, sheep, goats, and camels is overpowering. The true Hararis can be recognized by their women, who wear tight-fitting trousers in bright colors under their *shammas*, but the Galla predominate, an attractive people whose women wear their hair distinctively styled with two large buns at the side of the head, draped, usually, with leaves and flowers entwined into chains. The whole town has the air of a marketplace, and though no longer Moslem, is still Islamic in mood and color. It has its own language, Harari, but among the thousands tightly packed in its streets, you will hear the languages of the Amhara, the

Somalis, the Gallas, the Danakil, Shangalla, Sidamo, as well as Italian, Greek, French, English, and Arabic. Its population was never much more than thirty thousand or so; but this number, tightly packed within the confining walls, always gave the impression of a much higher density.

Now, having once more escaped the press of its sweating bodies, the Duke sat on the peaceful terrace of the café and stared moodily at his glass. Maria sat beside him and stroked his hand with her long, sensitive fingers.

He said gloomily: "Some bloody little peasant girl from the interior. She's probably never worn a pair of shoes in her life."

I said: "She might turn out to be a raving beauty."

He grimaced. "Hardly, dear boy." His English idiom was straight from London. "You don't know that part of the world, the bush she lives in. Nothing but goats. And in families that live on goats, the girls invariably look like them."

I glanced at Maria. She seemed to be amused at his discomfort. She was going off to see her family for a while, out of the way for the wedding, but she said cheerfully: "It will only be for a week or two, and by the time I get back all the fuss will be over and we'll be back to normal."

Her mixture of languages was crazy. She would start in English, then switch to Italian with a word or two of French thrown in, then back to English again: *"Due settimane per allontarmi, c'est assez, non e vero, qu'est-ce-que tu crois?* Two weeks is enough, no?"

Every time I saw Maria, she looked more beautiful; and more in love with her consort. There was an almost Phoenician cast to her features. She leaned over and patted him on the cheek and said: "I go for two weeks while you make love to your goat, and then I come back."

He smiled at her. "As soon as the chiefs have all gone back to their tribes and reported on the happy event . . ."

It was a perfectly normal state of affairs. Though technically

Christian, and allowed only one wife, any Ethiopian of consequence admitted that one woman could hardly be enough.
Concubines and servants filled in the gaps. And, somehow, I
had a feeling that the unknown little peasant girl might just
find a kind of happiness in the big, sprawling Palace of Harar;
once she got used to wearing dresses and high-heeled shoes.

It was a marriage of state, of course, negotiated by the
Emperor and his ministers with the rulers of the girl's tribe.
And until the wedding, neither the bride nor the groom would
see each other.

Meanwhile, Ato Waldo, as senior representative of the Emperor in this area, had taken over the arrangements for the
affair. He had sent his aide-de-camp to Paris to buy the trous-
seau. The wedding was to be a private matter, but the reception was something else again, and the Governor and I were
invited as the two senior representatives of the foreign power
that seemed so loath to leave their borders.

A slight and subtle move, perhaps; but it was an indication
that the facade of pretense was cracking, if only at this personal
and social level.

*　　*　　*

The Governor and I arrived, correctly, precisely one hour
after the time on the invitation. It was five o'clock in the
evening, and Reggie was resplendent in his dress uniform with
all the medals and decorations. He felt a little embarrassed,
because he was always happier when he could wear shorts and
an old shirt and just potter about. He didn't exactly fall over
his sword, but I expected him to at any minute. He whispered
anxiously: "Keep close to me all the time, I hate these things,
I never know what to say."

The huge reception hall had been draped with woven tapes-
tries that depicted incidents in Ethiopia's long, proud history.

Some had been painted on pale gray bark cloth, in reds and blues and greens and yellows. One of them was a series of sketches, in cartoon form, a nutshell history of Solomon's seduction of the Queen of Sheba, the first square showing their meeting, and the last depicting the two of them wrapped in a blanket and arranging for the birth of the infant Menelik.

The Queen, they firmly believe, visited King Solomon about 950 B.C. There is some biblical evidence to this effect in the First Book of Kings: *"Now when the Queen of Sheba heard of the fame of Solomon concerning the Lord, she came to test him with hard questions. She came to Jerusalem with a very great retinue, with camels bearing spices, and very much gold and precious stones . . . never again came such an abundance of spices as these which the Queen of Sheba gave to King Solomon."*

They believe in a charming legend concerning this encounter—and those spices. Solomon, they say, asked the lovely Queen to sleep with him, and she refused. She agreed, however, to pass the night in his room, and extracted a promise from him that he would lay no hand on her. But in this light persiflage between two mighty rulers, the king extracted his own promise—that she, during the night, would not steal any of his property.

He ordered his cooks to spice their evening meal heavily, and carefully neglected to have a *jara* of cool water placed by her bed. In the night, the Queen awoke with an intolerable thirst, found no water available, and crept close to the King's bed to drink from the *jara* he had just as carefully placed by his own bed.

Lying awake and waiting, he seized her, and accused her of "stealing" his water from him; her promise broken, his was no longer valid.

They slept together for the rest of the night, so the legend goes, and the resultant offspring was Menelik I, King of Ethiopia.

Sheba's homeland was the barren desert of Southern Arabia, so desolate that it is known today as the Rub el Khali, or Empty Quarter, flanked on the south by the harsh mountains of Yemen (her palace was probably near San'a, Yemen's capital) and on the north by half a million square miles of waterless sand dunes. But it lay across the route from the Malay Archipelago and India to Egypt and the Mediterranean, and her Sabaen Kingdom derived its immense wealth from the trade between these varied centers of contemporary civilization.

It was from this area, also, that the Ethiopians were believed, originally, to have migrated.

I studied the bark-cloth cartoons, richly painted in brilliant reds and blues and greens, each square telling its own individual part of the historical legend, as more and more of the guests arrived, by car, by camel, by mule, and on horseback, escorted along the garden paths by guards who carried umbrellas to shade them from the evening sun.

Some of the court officials wore neat European suits and dark glasses, and others were dressed in the more traditional white *shamma*. There was food and drink everywhere, in enormous quantities, and the air was ripe with the scent of incense. Soon, it would be smoked up with burning candles too; there was electricity in the palace, but it didn't often work.

The palace was high on a hill overlooking the town, with bright red bougainvillea and honeysuckle everywhere, and carved arabesque ornamentation in white stone, and tall trees that were dark green against the bright blue sky. It was a building of great antiquity, and of immense character and charm.

The wedding ceremony had long been over, and the guests were tightly packed in the huge reception chamber. The Duke sat on his gold throne and welcomed us as we moved in, one by one, and bowed. The major-domo intoned our names as we approached the throne, more than a thousand of us filing past. The Duke grinned at Reggie and said: "I'm afraid all this will bore you terribly, Your Excellency. But do please be patient with us." He looked at me and said: "Nice to see you here, Major."

But I couldn't take my eyes off his bride. Without exception, she was the most lovely young woman I'd ever set eyes on. She was little more than a child (in her kind of society, ages were never known very precisely), but she carried herself like a queen with a regal dignity that was quite astonishing; I thought of the Duke's misgivings about her.

Her cheekbones were high, her eyes large and slanted, and her skin was the *capucino* brown that is so highly prized by the Ethiopians. (They believe that the lighter a woman's skin, the cooler it is on a hot night. Conversely, the black women of the coastal areas were as highly prized by the Arabs across the Red Sea and to the north, for precisely the same reason. The trade in slaves, many of them women, across the Bab el Mandeb, the "Gate of Tears," that separates the two continents by a mere twenty miles of water, was always a two-way business.)

The young Duchess' features were perfect, her nose straight and fine, her eyebrows highly arched. Her hair was piled high on her head in three concentric waves, one above the other, and fastened with intricately carved ebony pins. The dress that Ato Waldo had brought from Paris was shimmering white and tight-fitting on a slender, willowy body with high-jutting breasts and an almost nonexistent waist.

The girls here mature very early, and she could not have been more than fifteen years old, but there was a wise and mischievous light in those huge eyes that was really quite tantalizing. It was as though she knew, quite well, the impression she was making, not only on her husband but on all the guests as well.

163

The long line was breaking up, and I looked at Reggie. We hung around, smiling and nodding and bowing on occasion as chiefs and nobles and the ordinary gentry made their courtly little obeisances to us, and I noticed that the two of us were the only Englishmen there. There was a Greek trader named Parakis, and the Armenian trader Hadkinjian, and the mysterious Pole with the opaque monocle who called himself Count Vilaski. But the others were all Ethiopians, the staff of the palace, the Duke's personal friends, the tribal chiefs from the surrounding country, and some from up north where the girl's family lived. A priest passed by, swinging his silver burner, intoning a blessing on us all.

Ato Waldo, when the line had come to an end, proposed an elaborate toast to the bride and groom. And it is indicative of his fine sense of courtesy that the involved ritual of the toast was carefully repeated in English, for our benefit, and in French for the other three Europeans. We drank their health in Royal *tej*—and how different this was from the run-of-the-mill stuff, smooth and warm as old Amontillado!

The servants were bustling about in bare, noiseless feet, holding out tiny trays of food with both hands, in the accepted manner, bowing as they served us and slipping quickly away for refills. There was chicken, and goat, and slices of raw and cooked beef, and a dozen different kinds of cheeses. There was roast pheasant, and braised partridge, and stuffed suckling pig, and a huge barbecued lamb, all set out on tables with row upon row of bottles of *tej*, whisky, gin, and beer. There was a horrible soft drink that Hadkinjian made out of pomegranates, and there was enough champagne to float a battleship. Great blocks of ice had been laid out on tables in strategic corners, ice from the factory down in Dire-Daua, and from time to time, when the electricity unexpectedly came on for a while, the fans would play over them and blow cool air all over the room.

I congratulated Ato Waldo on the success of his reception,

and he made a polite little bow and said: "A great occasion, an occasion we have all been waiting for."

The groom was circulating, chatting briefly with the guests while his bride—who spoke only her local dialect and a smattering of Amharic—sat on her throne and waited.

And at last, it was time for the consummation.

A few small speeches were made, the priest went on his rounds with his incense burner again, and the young bride was escorted by the older women of her family to the bedroom. In a few moments, the Duke waved a cheerful hand at us, and joined her.

I found Reggie at the bar, drinking Marie Brizzard Anisette, one of his favorite drinks.

He couldn't get over his astonishment at the sight of the young bride. Like almost any other country, Ethiopia has its share of beautiful women, and its share of ugly ones too; but some of them have a grace of carriage that is quite startling, and features that are lovely by any standard, even the most demanding. And this young child-woman would have turned heads in the world's most sophisticated capitals.

He said, whispering: "What a lucky choice they made for him! She's absolutely gorgeous."

I said: "And he was rather expecting a goat. He saw her for the first time today."

"Well, I'm delighted for him. He's such a nice man. I have a feeling that the consummation might not be quite the hurried affair we all expected."

"Do they produce a blood-stained sheet here?"

Among the Arabs, the Somalis, the Galla, and some of the Hararis, it is customary for proof of the bride's virginity to be shown to the assembled guests. Sometimes, the sheet is stained with the blood of a chicken whose throat has been ceremonially cut, so that the polite fiction is maintained whatever the anatomical circumstances may be.

Reggie shook his head. "No, I don't think so. But I'm not sure, and I don't like to ask."

"No, we'd better not. And do we have to wait till he comes out of the bedroom? I believe that's the proper thing. Or can we leave at midnight?"

The Governor fidgeted with his glass, and said at last: "I think we really ought not.to leave before Ato Waldo. Let's take our cue from him, would that be correct?"

"As long as you're not the first or the last to go, I don't suppose it matters very much."

He was horrified. He said quickly: "But it matters a great deal! We must choose the right moment very carefully. About ten or fifteen minutes *after* Ato Waldo would be about right."

I said carefully, knowing that it was a touchy subject: "That would give him a certain advantage of authority, is that what you want?"

"Yes, that's what I want." He was beaming now, very pleased with himself. He said: "First of all, we're on his territory now, indisputably, and secondly, if we honor the occasion correctly now, then we can put him in his place again next time we see him." He peered at me and said: "There is no precedent for this sort of thing, of course, but you do think I'm right, don't you? Don't you?"

I said: "I'm sure you're perfectly right."

He was hopelessly out of place in the world of protocol; and protocol here was immensely important. In other diplomatic circles, an error in propriety would merely be distasteful, but here it could easily arouse very angry passions, and it was really essential to behave as we were expected to behave.

He said, whispering delightedly, a broad smile in his eyes: "Remember Theodore's letter."

It was less than seventy years ago that a relatively trifling breach of diplomatic etiquette had led to a brief but brutal war with England, in which Ethiopia suffered one of her very rare military defeats . . .

The then King of Ethiopia, Theodore, had sent a letter to the Queen of England which had not been answered promptly enough to satisfy his well-developed sense of what was right. Indeed, it had never been answered at all; some clerk in the Foreign Office had merely pigeonholed it.

King Theodore, the *Negus Negusti*, or King of Kings, had been so enraged by this affront to his dignity that he had seized the British Consul, Captain Cameron, together with all his staff, and had flung them into prison. Two missionaries, and the wife of one of them, had been arrested with the consular staff, and were flogged and horribly tortured.

Word of these actions had reached London, and after abortive attempts to free the captives diplomatically, a military expedition was sent out to rescue them by force; twelve thousand troops—four thousand British and eight thousand Indian —under General Sir Robert Napier, a highly skilled professional soldier who later became known as Napier of Magdala.

His army landed at Annesy Bay on the Red Sea, made a rapid forced march into Ethiopia in the face of enormous difficulties—notably, the supply of water—and met the Ethiopians in battle at Magdala on the plain of Arogi.

The battle was a massacre. In the short time at his disposal, Theodore could muster only some three thousand men, armed with musket-loading rifles and spears, and they were rapidly decimated by the more modern arms of the British.

And when the invaders reached the palace of Magdala and bombarded it, the King shot himself on its steps at the moment of their entry, rather than submit to them.

Now, perhaps, the times had changed; but how much?

It was easy to forget, in the casual exchange of small talk, that these were a people who really still lived in a semi-barbaric past. *"The unique specimen,"* the historian H. F. Tozer had written, *"of a semi-barbarous Christian people."* Barbarity is a word that permits of many interpretations; perhaps there is more of it in America and in Europe than in Ethiopia. Nonetheless, the passions were strong here, and easily aroused. Honor is a concept that is less important to us than it used to be. Not so here; the courtly manners could only color, not hide, the latent fierceness that could always be seen in those dark, composed eyes.

"We don't want another incident like that, do we?" the Governor whispered.

I said mildly: "They don't change as fast as we do, I know. But I hardly think there's any of that sort of danger."

"No, neither do I. But I'd hate to be proved wrong, wouldn't you?"

Their power here was absolute, in the sense that a lion rules absolutely in the bush, with absolute indifference to the intruder—unless he is disturbed.

There is a great affinity between the lion and the Ethiopian. One of the Emperor's titles is The Lion of Judah.

I wandered off and chatted for a while with some of the guests, and had a lot to drink and a great deal to eat, and at midnight I found Ato Waldo and talked with him. We discussed the sad state of the road between Harar and Dire-Daua, which had been laid like a ribbon up the steep side of the mountains by the Italians, a breathtaking road of violent hairpin bends and sheer drops down to the rocks a thousand feet below; it had never been repaired since the Italians had gone, and was falling away alarmingly in places. And then I looked at my watch and said: "Are you returning to Dire-Daua tonight?"

He smiled and shrugged and made a little gesture. "It all depends. I can't leave, of course, until His Highness returns to us after the consummation. I do not know when that will be."

"Then we might be here all night. If I have any more to eat or drink, they'll have to wheel me home."

He said cheerfully: "There are beds and couches in some of the other rooms." I wondered if he knew something I didn't.

I wandered over to Reggie and said glumly: "The grapevine has it that we might be here all night."

"Oh dear. Armina will be terribly worried." He looked about for Vilaski and Parakis, who were arguing vehemently in a corner by themselves. As though assuring himself that his ideas on protocol were right—and, to be truthful, they were—he nodded and said: "And *they* can't go until *we* do. . . . I found some Guinness, would you like a Black Velvet?"

Guinness? In Harar?

I said: "They must have brought it in especially for you."

"Yes, yes, I know that." Beaming, he poured me a half-glass of Guinness and filled it up with champagne, then made himself another. He said: "And I really think we ought to circulate a little more, don't you?"

We moved off independently, and made small talk, and kept looking at our watches. I sat in a comfortable armchair and half-slept for a while, and when daylight came made another assault on the food. I noticed that fresh supplies were being brought in constantly, as though the servants had been alerted for a long siege.

We wandered around, and chatted from time to time, and dozed a little more, and in the early afternoon I broached once more the subject of leaving.

I said to Reggie: "Everybody is still here, everybody, every single one of them. And two more truckloads of food just arrived."

The Governor shook his head. "We all have to wait. The Duke will appear, we'll all congratulate him, and then Ato Waldo will be the first to go. After that, you and I, and then the other Europeans. The others will wait for an hour or so, and then start to leave in diminishing order of importance." He shook his head, worrying about it: "I told Armina I might be late getting home, but . . . but this . . ."

Ato Waldo, our cue to go, was sitting on a divan, patiently fanning himself with an ostrich-feather fan. I walked past him and smiled, and bowed, and he smiled and bowed his head deeply in return. There was a movement over by the bedroom door, but it was only food being taken in to the young lovers, and I knew that if they were eating in there we'd still be hanging around for some time yet.

Night came, and then the next morning.

I found Reggie asleep on a sofa, and he opened his eyes wide and said: "Ah, good, they've come out?"

I said gloomily: "Not yet."

He nodded and went back to sleep.

I located a bed and slept for a while in my uniform, wishing I had a change of clothes. I found a tub, and a servant to fill it for me, and took a quick bath, hoping I wouldn't be caught short by the couple's emergence while I was absent and naked, and had some more to eat and drink when I came back to the reception hall.

The guests were all still there, every one of them, scattered over the various rooms and waiting. Some of them slept, some ate, some wandered around; there was a lot of surreptitious looking at wristwatches. Only Ato Waldo seemed composed and patient. I saw food being taken in to the consummation room again, and dishes being removed; but nobody came out.

The night came and went, and another and another. And, on the next morning, the door was flung open and His Highness the Duke made his ceremonial return at last; he seemed surprised to find us all still there. We clapped our hands and gathered round him, and offered him our felicitations.

The consummation had lasted just seven hours short of five days.

13

The lions around Jig-Jigga were getting bolder. It was as though they were openly showing their contempt for the admittedly insufficient steps I had taken against them.

I had ordered free ammunition to be given to the best hunters in the area, put a bounty on the lions' heads, and taken the ban off the manufacture of arrow poison. Inspector Tafeta had been organizing periodic hunts, and we had assisted the outlying Somalis in the construction of heavy thorn barriers, called *zeribas,* around their *rers.*

All around the town, these *rers*—a single hut, or a dozen or more of them, spotted here and there over the gently rolling hills—had been put down from time to time by the nomadic Somalis of the desert. The camels that went along with these families would graze on the sparse gray scrub, and when it was all gone, the huts would be dismantled, their poles and skins loaded on the camels' backs, and fresh pastures would be sought out.

If they were staying for any length of time in one place, a *zeriba* was mandatory; but where the scrub was dried out and might last only a few days, it was hardly worth the effort of cutting the thorn branches and dragging them into position, and it was on these outlying, unprotected *rers* that the man-eaters were preying.

They were not always successful. On many occasions they had been driven off by Somali slings or the concerted effort of their spears. But this was not enough; they had to be killed.

I called Sir Reginald for help. He knew more of the habits of lions than any man I had ever met, particularly the bush lion of his beloved Somaliland.

We drove down to the Ogaden together in his big old Dodge, with Lucertola at the wheel, and called a conference with Inspector Tafeta, Jig-Jigga's best hunting man. And the Governor sent out runners to the outlying *rers* to bring in the area's best trackers.

The Somali tracker is a legend. He can tell at once from quite invisible marks in the hard-packed sand whether the woman who left them was carrying a load of firewood on her head—or was merely pregnant; they can tell you who passed where, and how long ago; they can tell by studying the tracks of camels, going both ways, in which direction the water lies.

And by late afternoon of the first day, some thirty trackers and beaters arrived, armed with their spears and the deadly slings which they crack like rifles and with which they can stun a lion by a single hurled stone, fast as a bullet, between the eyes.

As children, we were taught that David, a young shepherd-boy, killed Goliath of Gath with a sling, and we wondered about it.

Later on, we came to realize that it might not have been the young shepherd at all, but rather the Hebrew warrior Elhanan, and that even if it *were* David, he might have been considerably older and already the armor-bearer to King Saul and consequently a man of some martial ability.

But the earlier fancy remains with us. The Judean tradition states that *"David put his hand into a bag, and took thence a stone, and slung it, and smote the Philistine in his forehead, that the stone sunk into his forehead; and he fell upon his face to the earth."* It also records that the shepherd-boy had already killed a lion and a bear with his sling, when they attacked his sheep.

And the sling, indeed, is an arm of considerable consequence. It is not, in the hands of a camel herder, a toy to be played with. It consists of two leather thongs, some three feet long, joined by the flat leather pouch which holds the stone— usually about the size of a golf ball. It is swung around the thrower's head six, seven, nine times, gathering a tremendous velocity as it winds up. One thong is let go, with the sharp, incisive crack of a bullwhip, and the stone hurtles toward its target with a velocity—and accuracy—that can only be described as frightening.

It is slower in use, of course, than a rifle. But it has a longer range than a spear or even a Somali bow. It is easy to make, and hard to use. The missiles themselves are always readily available. And in the hands of an expert, the sling is a highly efficient and deadly weapon.

They came to us now, the slingmen. Moving in a long, slow line through the thickets, they would act as our beaters. And the lions, we knew, would leave their hiding places to run from those deadly sounds.

We mapped the outlying *rers* where the lions had been seen, and noted particularly where they had made their kills—an old woman here, a child there, a man returning from his camel driving somewhere else. We tried to find some sort of pattern.

173

Tafeta said: "They seem to move clockwise every night." He stubbed a hand on the sketch he had made of the territory, and said: "Here, ten days ago, that's where they took the young boy. The next night, they moved over here, and killed another child. The next night I set up a blind and waited for them here, but they bypassed me and moved over to here."

Sir Reginald said, quite sure of it: "One old lion, at least, who knows that the pride is being hunted, is that the pattern?"

Tafeta agreed. His voice was soft and low and gentle, an unlikely voice for such a bear of a man. He said: "Yes, I'd say that's true. Most of the kills seem to have been made by one very big animal, I'd say ten or twelve years old, but there's at least one case where the victim, a woman who was asleep outside the *rer*, was taken by one of the younger ones, probably a two- or three-year-old, from the size of the pad marks. There are five of them altogether. One undisputed leader, the big one."

The Somalis sat around us on the ground, their spears stuck up between their bony knees, not really liking the fact that Tafeta, an Ethiopian, was heading the hunt, but putting up with it for the sake of the Governor.

Sir Reginald said: "All right, tonight."

He put a small stone in the geographical center of the sketch and said: "Tafeta to the north, you take the south, I'll take the west. We'd better send two or three Somalis out in each direction to look for tracks so that we can take the trail at first light if we don't find them during the darkness—or if they don't find us. Jig-Jigga is on the east, so the police patrols can be doubled up and sent to the outskirts to keep them out of the town and in our general area. What about blinds?"

Tafeta said promptly: "I've had six of them built, in the most likely places. All we have to do is move into them, take along a few goats to tether as bait. Here, here, two more on the slope of this hill, one on the top, and another by the side of the dry riverbed."

"Good. The trackers had better spend the night up in the hills, can we find them a *rer* to sleep in? With a good thorn fence around it?"

He spoke rapid Somali to the head tracker, and decided on a small *rer* to the west of the Madar Pass. From here, they would fan out in the first light of the early morning and plot the lions' tracks.

And just as the sun was nearing the horizon, and the sand was a brilliant red gold, we set out in our trucks in three different directions.

Tafeta headed north, Sir Reginald drove himself to the *rer* where he would drop off his load of Somalis, and I, with the farthest to go—seven miles—set off alone in the old Ford truck that was our standby transportation here.

The life expectancy of a good truck in these parts is not much more than a few months; after that, you keep it together with rope, ingenuity, and whatever spare parts you can cannibalize from other abandoned trucks left out in the deserts. Supplies, so soon after the war, were very hard to come by, and this old Ford, with five or six years of military service behind it before we liberated it, was a disaster. But it would go, and that was all that really mattered. As usual, we had to push it to get it started, because the battery was quite flat, and I made a mental note to park it on the slope of the hill so that I could start it again in the morning.

The plain, as I drove across it, was teeming with game. There were hundreds of Thomson gazelle, a group of gerenuk, a big herd of zebra, forty or fifty gnus morosely browsing, a galloping herd of more than three hundred hyenas—coming out a little early, I thought—a few ostrich, some impalas, an oryx, and quite a lot of the tiny *dik-dik,* the mouse deer, that stood no more than eight inches high at the shoulder. I saw a family of wild boar, and when I reached the high ground, grass covered now, where I hoped to find my blind, I saw a family of giant kudu standing majestically on the skyline; they took off at my approach, heading down into the valley below.

The blind, surprisingly, was exactly where it was supposed to be. It consisted of thirty or forty mangrove poles—ironwood so strong it cannot be cut with a saw—sunk deeply into the ground in the form of a cage, about eight feet square. The poles were about ten inches apart, and one of them had been left loose to provide entrance. Tafeta had thoughtfully provided a water bag which was tied to one corner and was slowly leaking into the sand, a large goatskin shining with damp and cool to the touch.

I eased myself inside and settled down. I took the goat in with me, but it stubbornly refused to make any noise, and its bleating was essential to attract the pride, so I took it out again in the darkness and tethered it, whereupon it set up a ceaseless wailing that went on all through the night.

The silence, apart from that sound, was uncanny. Once or twice it would be broken by the pounding of hyenas' hooves, sounding like galloping horses as they raced over the grass, and once it was broken by their frightening mad-woman shriek as they found their carrion food somewhere out there.

I kept absolutely quiet, and waited, and nothing happened at all, and at daylight I climbed out through the bars again, retrieved my miserable goat, and carried it to where I had left the truck, on the side of the hill about a quarter of a mile away. The gasoline tank was leaking slightly, and there was the sour stench of gas in the air. I removed the stone I had put under the front wheel, jumped aboard as it rolled down the hill, threw in the clutch to start it, and one hour later I was back in Jig-Jigga.

The others came back empty-handed too, and when we held

a meeting with the trackers in the late afternoon, we learned that the pride had skillfully avoided all the blinds, had moved down into the riverbed, and had killed a man who had been sleeping outside his solitary *rer*. They had dragged in the remains of the body to show us—once more, the two tiny holes at the side of the skull, and the body eaten from the feet upward, to the hip on one side, to the shoulder on the other. The head, again, had been left intact except for those two tiny holes. The legend is that the lion leaves the head for the *macmiss* bird, a large black crow that will follow a lion all through the bush, calling out: *"macmiss . . . macmiss . . . macmiss."* to lead the hunter to his prey—or the prey to the hunter. The hunter, too, is supposed to leave the lion's head for the bird, and if he is a Mitgan, that is what he will do.

We went back to the blinds at dark for another sleepless night, and once again, our patience was unrewarded. The third night and the fourth were the same, and in that period two more people were taken; but on the fifth night, I came in close, and very alarming, contact with one of the pride—the ten-year-old male that Tafeta had spoken of.

I had left the truck a lot farther away this time, since it occurred to me that its smell was too strong and might alarm the pride. I had left it parked on a very steep hill with a big round boulder just under one of the wheels, and had walked about a mile to get into position. I was squatting on the sand in my cage and listening, and it was about three o'clock in the morning when the sound of the goat's bleating suddenly stopped.

There was no moon. It was black as pitch.

I strained my eyes and could see nothing, and the silence seemed to be pounding in my ears; it was unbelievably still and quiet. My flashlight was strapped to the barrel of my Lee-Enfield—the rifle the Governor had always objected to—and so fastened that the aiming point was dead center of the circle of light it threw, but I dared not switch it on until I knew that I had a target.

Nothing.

No sound or sight of any kind, and yet I was quite sure that something was out there in the darkness. I didn't know whether the goat was alive or dead, and it was only twenty feet away from me. You are supposed to get your single killing shot in before the bait is taken—a question of a hunter's professional pride—and I was already beginning to feel that I had been outwitted.

For a long, long time I waited. I did not want to move, even to look at the luminous hands of my watch, but I must have crouched there and waited for ten or fifteen minutes, or maybe a great deal more.

And then, with a blow that almost knocked me out of my crouch, that *something* thudded itself into the bars of my cage, and I heard one of the ironwood poles shatter with a sudden, frightening crash, all the more alarming because it was quite unexpected. I threw myself sideways, away from the blow, and swung round my rifle and switched on the light, and there, right on top of me, but on the other side of the bars, was the lion, no more than a few feet away. The gun fired, an instinctive reflex, and even as it went off I knew that I had not centered the light and that I had missed.

How can you miss so large a target at such close range? It's quite easy. I was caught up in a broken pole, its jagged end jutting into my stomach, and my only impulse was to get a shot off fast, if only to drive him away. I was off balance and I fell, and when I turned over quickly to get my second shot in, there was nothing in the bright circle of light but a dead goat.

The lion had gone. I had not heard him come, I had not heard him make his kill, and I had not heard him race off into the darkness.

I must admit that I was shaken. There had not been even

the smell of him to warn me. Upwind, of course; I wouldn't have expected anything else.

When daylight came, I inspected the broken pole; five inches thick, and it had been snapped in two like a matchstick. I searched for blood marks but found none—my shot, as I feared, had gone quite wild—and I reflected that perhaps this was a good thing; there's nothing more deadly than a man-eating lion except one that has been wounded. And again, it's another point of honor among African hunters that an animal is either killed, with a single shot, or left alone; to wound an animal and let it escape is considered a very bad thing indeed, and rightly so.

I walked slowly over to the truck, and kicked at the stone under the wheel to free it. It wouldn't budge. I put my rifle aboard, in the gun rack, and tackled the boulder with both hands. It still wouldn't move.

The rock was heavy, about two feet across, and it had rolled into place easily enough when I had put it there. But during the night the wheel had settled on it more firmly, so after repeated attempts to free it, I took my bush knife and cut a small thorn-tree branch and used it as a lever, and after some five or six minutes of fruitless effort, the branch snapped in two and I gave up.

I found some twigs and made a fire, and brewed myself some coffee, and drank a couple of bottles of beer that were wrapped in wet sacking at the back of the truck to keep them cool, and then went back to work. I found the jack (faintly surprised that there was one), and jacked up the offending wheel to the maximum height, and then rolled the boulder out of the way.

And at that precise moment, the truck rolled forward off the jack and crashed down with a thud onto all four wheels once more. I twisted sideways to get out of its way, and lay there on the ground, waiting for it to stop.

But it didn't, and by the time I jumped to my feet it was

a hundred feet ahead of me and moving fast, and gaining speed too. I raced after it, but the slope was considerable, and the distance between us increased rapidly as it bumped and careened over the broken ground.

Less than a hundred yards ahead, the edge of the plain gave way suddenly, in a slow and stately drop of smooth, hard sand that went on for miles and finally came to the edge of the Madar Pass itself—a drop of several hundred feet over a sheer cliff. I kept running, as fast as I could, but I knew that I'd seen the last of the truck, and finally I gave up.

By the time I was completely out of breath, the truck was just as completely out of sight; it had veered to one side, and the last I saw of it, it was heading for the lip of the gorge at some forty miles an hour, rolling easily over the flat, unobstructed desert.

I wondered if we would ever see it again, and where I could find a replacement if indeed it was going over the edge; but soon I fell into the lackadaisical African state of mind in which nothing really matters. Even the loss of my rifle presented no problem; it was merely a matter of sending a patrol out the next day to look for it and for whatever might be left of the vehicle. (They found the truck, the next evening, lying at the bottom of the pass on its side, a total wreck.)

I didn't feel, I remember, as foolish as perhaps I should have. Things like this seem to happen all the time in Africa, and the really important thing is that nobody ever worries about them.

On the contrary, out there alone in the silent foothills, with the high mountains behind me and the great plain of the Ogaden stretching out into infinity, I felt very much on top of the world—a state of euphoria brought on by the feeling of detachment that goes with solitude in the desert. It was like being home again, in the middle of the Sahara, with nothing in sight or sound as far as a man's imaginings could reach.

There's nothing quite as satisfying as the early morning in

the bush, with the kind of clean air we don't seem to breathe much of any more, the wind slight and cool, and the bushes still heavy with the night's dew, and glistening brightly.

I was only seven miles or so from home, which in those parts is not much of a walk, so I set off back to Jig-Jigga in good spirits. I even started phrasing the story I would have to tell of the lion that broke the mangrove pole with one swipe of his paw . . .

It was seven o'clock in the morning now, beautifully clear and fresh. The shadows of the tall acacias were still long and slender across the red sand as I went down toward the plain. I took off my bush jacket as the sun climbed higher, and tucked it into my belt. I wondered how the others had fared during the night.

And then—then, I smelled him.

I felt my scalp prickling first, and wondered momentarily what was wrong, and then there was that distinct, downwind lion smell, so strong that I knew he was dangerously close by.

I stopped in my tracks and looked around. I studied every bush, every shrub in sight. I even looked hard at the tiny patches of shadow the cactus plants were throwing, for a lion, it sometimes seems, can hide under the head of a pin.

I could not find him.

I started to walk on slowly again, my heart in my mouth, and very conscious that there was no tree in sight in which I could take shelter, even if that would have been a help, which it wouldn't. There was nothing I could do but keep moving.

And then I saw him. He was standing quite out in the open, scorning cover, not more than fifty feet away—one of those tricks your eyes play on you when you are looking for something a few hundred yards away and it's right under your nose all the time. He was so close that I almost yelped.

His tawny skin merged perfectly with the sand, and I realized that I must have looked right through him a couple of times while I was searching greater distances. His tail was flicking gently from side to side—a danger sign—and he was looking right at me.

I turned away. There's nothing that makes a lion more angry, and faster, than staring at him. The theory is that if you leave him alone, he's harmless, and not staring is part of the leaving alone. You're also safe, the theory goes, if he's just eaten, but I didn't like to look long enough to see if his belly was full or not.

And whether or not it was the same lion I had shot at during the night—or even one of the man-eating pride—I had no way of knowing. All I could do was keep on moving, quite slowly. I was terrified.

I loosened the strap of my hunting knife, the only weapon I had, but I knew too that this was useless. A man can fight a leopard with a knife, or even with his bare hands if he's strong and agile enough and can keep out of the way of the ripping hind paws that try to tear his stomach out, but against a lion there is nothing that can be done. (Even with a leopard, an unarmed encounter will leave you crippled for life.)

Most people do not realize the frightening strength of a wild animal, particularly a lion, the strongest of them all. I once saw a young male take a half-grown cow in his jaws, toss it over his back, and leap a ten-foot-high thorn fence with it. I had seen what a lion could do, just a few hours earlier, with an "unbreakable" ironwood pole. They will bring down a five-hundred-pound wildebeest with the impetus of a sixty-foot leap. Their casual strength, quite effortless, is phenomenal, and if you are attacked, when you are unarmed, all you can do is die gracefully.

I moved steadily away.

He was still standing there, unconcerned with me or with anything else, just looking at me with a mild sort of interest. And then he began to move toward me, and I had to fight the impulse to run—the worst thing to do under such circumstances. He came on, as I walked, and slowly padded along beside me, so close that I could easily have touched him, and I don't think I have ever been so frightened in my life.

He was absolutely silent, his great paws treading rhythmically on the soft sand without the faintest whisper of sound, and his shoulder muscles seemed to quiver loosely under that yellow silky skin as he moved along in awesome majesty, a foot from my side, like a dog out for a walk with its master.

It must have been for fifteen minutes that he held his position, and then he wandered off to investigate a patch of shadow, and I desperately searched the horizon for a tree that I could climb; there was nothing. Then he started moving in once more, and he came within reach of my fingers again and walked beside me, not doing anything, not even looking at me, just scaring the daylights out of me by merely being there.

I could see the dirt road now, half a mile ahead of me, and he was still close by my side. Jig-Jigga lay a thousand yards along the road, to the right, round a bluff in the deep red sandstone. I realized I would have to make a right turn to get there, and that's the side he was on.

And when we came to the road, he was still there, not more than a couple of feet from my bare knees. I was beginning to think of them not as knees any more, but as gammon.

I turned to the right, wondering if this were going to be my big mistake. I passed within a few inches of his nose, and if he had yawned I think I would have dropped dead there and then. I tried to persuade myself that it was just the neighbor's dog watching me go by, but it didn't help. He stood on the piled sand at the edge of the road, his forelegs a little higher than his rear, one hind leg stretched back and his tail moving slowly from side to side—that danger sign again, the sign that he's going to charge.

But he didn't. He just stood there and looked at me

morosely, looking for all the world like a magazine illustration of the King of Beasts, his head held up and slightly turned. It was an unbelievably noble attitude. My mouth was as dry as dust.

And when I reached the sandstone bluff and saw the little market town ahead of me, with the crowds already pouring in to the square, I risked a look back to see if he was still there. He was. He seemed to be the friendliest creature in the bush.

And when I reached the outskirts, I looked back once more. He was gone.

The others had been more fortunate than I had.

During the long night, they'd seen nothing. And the lions took another man the following night. We decided to hunt them down by day.

*   *   *

It was now our seventh day in Jig-Jigga, and we had gotten nowhere.

But the Somali trackers had mapped for us a very comprehensive picture of the lions' movements, and we were able to estimate, with a fair degree of certainty, where we might be able to find them during their daylight resting hours.

We set off toward the valley where we thought they might be hiding—the Governor, Inspector Tafeta, myself, and a dozen or so of the beaters.

Halfway up the steep grassy slope where I had lost the truck, Sir Reginald looked off to one side toward a small, solitary Somali *rer,* and said: "A *fal,* a soothsayer, let's find out what he has to say." He translated, and the Somalis nodded their approval.

We walked over and stood the traditional fifty paces from the hut, bent bamboo poles over which animal skins were tightly stretched, and called out the mandatory *"Hodi!"* which is a warning for any women inside to cover their faces, and talked together loudly for a while, also mandatory, to let the inhabitants know that there were strangers around, and at last the old *fal* came out.

He was incredibly old, and wrinkled, and white haired, and bent with the burden of age. In all probability he was no more than sixty, but the age expectancy here is very short. He would have lived all his life on a diet of camels' milk, with never a piece of meat, which would be unclean for him, or a mess of sweet potatoes, which he would regard as infidels' food, to vary the monotony of his diet. His ribs were the ribs of a mummy, his skin like parchment or a long-dead leaf. His teeth had all gone, and he helped himself along with his spear.

We greeted him ceremoniously, passed the time of day, asked after his camels, his sons, and his family—in that order —and at last sat on the sand in a semicircle round him. The Governor, who spoke Somali a lot better than the old man himself, told him the purpose of our visit: we were out after lion—would we make a kill that day?

The old man nodded his head wisely, and after a moment he got up and hobbled inside his tent. When he came out again he was carrying a round wooden bowl, a piece of charcoal, two seashells, and a small stick bound with elephant hair.

He placed the bowl carefully on the sand, put the pieces of charcoal in the center of it, and poured sand over it with the seashells. Then he smoothed out the sand, and with the point of his skinny finger drew a few lines. He looked up at the sun. He drew some more lines. And finally he sat back on his haunches and closed his eyes.

He sat like this for a long, long time. Once, I started to speak, but the Governor looked up sharply and silenced me with a gesture. I looked at the faces of the trackers and saw that they were peering intently into the wooden bowl as if mesmerized. Tafeta, the Coptic Christian Ethiopian, a civilized man who could speak six languages, was quietly, quizzically watching the *fal*. I could sense his wondering if we believed all this —and if he ought to believe it himself.

Then, at last, the old man stood up, spoke quickly for a minute or so, using his slim old hands as eloquently as a ballerina, then turned and went abruptly into the tent. The trackers were nodding among themselves, scratching their heads, and looking a little puzzled.

I said to the Governor: "What was that all about?"

He said: "Well, according to the *fal*, and they're always right, you know, we shall not see the last of the lions until they have taken eleven people."

"Does that mean we'll shoot them, or not?"

He shook his head: "I don't know." He was frowning. "What he actually said was: 'You will see them go.' . . . Yes, that's the only way it can be translated, you will see them go when they have taken eleven people."

"So he wasn't very helpful, was he?"

"I don't know. It's very puzzling." He looked at Tafeta and asked: "How many have they taken so far?"

"Nine, sir."

I said: "Would everybody know that?"

He shook his head. "No, I don't think so. We've made an official count, of course, but nobody else is likely to go to that trouble. Up here in the hills, all they know is that some lions have turned man-eater."

Sir Reginald was frowning darkly, puzzling something out, and he said: "The Somali word he used for seeing them go . . . it really presupposes being *asked* to leave, or being . . . *chased away*. Not a very common phrase for the bush Somali to use. Yes, he really said: you will see them being chased away. Strange, I wonder what he meant?"

We found out during the evening.

All through the long day, the Somali beaters crossed and

recrossed a dense thicket where the tracks showed that the lions had entered and not gone out. They cracked their slings in an attempt to drive them out, and nothing happened. We went through ourselves, time and time again, and examined the prints and knew that they were in there somewhere, in among the thorny bushes and the tangled vines, four or five of them in an area of not much more than a dozen acres, but thick enough to be almost impenetrable.

Somewhere in there, they were hiding out—we were sure. And then, toward the evening, Tafeta and the Governor found a small strip of hard sandstone, hard enough to leave no tracks, and they called in the Somalis and examined it. Their leader, at last, nodded his head and said: "Yes it's possible . . ." They argued for a while in Somali, and the Governor, translating, said: "A spit of hard land just a few feet wide. It's possible, they agree, that they could have come out. We've wasted another day."

He was getting impatient now. He said in desperation: "Let's make one more run-through, we'll take as straight a line as we can, all of us, and cover every damned inch of it."

We fought our way through it, using our machetes, and found nothing.

Dispirited, we went back to town to rest up, and learning that early in the morning three young men who were searching for water had been attacked; two of them had been able to make their escape—while the lions were eating the third. Five of them, the survivors told us, led by a large and elderly male.

He was the tenth.

The next day, we started over. We beat through the thicket again, and followed tracks that were quite clear in the soft sand, well up into the hills that towered over the borders of the Madar Pass, all of us spread out with our rifles ready.

And then, toward four o'clock in the afternoon, the sun still beating down heavily, we heard a loud and totally unexpected sound, the sound of clashing drums, like a hundred kettledrums being beaten over there in the pass somewhere.

And as we stared in astonishment, a long thin line of men came slowly over the rise, two, three, four hundred of them, all along the horizon, spread out in a single line. They were banging at empty gasoline cans as they moved slowly toward us. They were perhaps two thousand yards away, and they were Ethiopian soldiers—*their* soldiers.

The Governor had a look of absolute horror on his face.

The hill marked the border of their territory and ours, and they were indubitably over on our side, and I could see all the vast structure of protocol and diplomatic ethics crumbling around him.

There was a single horseman with them, cantering easily from side to side ahead of the line, and I said: "Whatever you say, Reggie. Do you want me to go and see what they're up to?"

He was spluttering his indignation: "But they're soldiers! In *our* territory! In full uniform! Good God Almighty!"

Tafeta looked worried. He said: "Of course, they may not realize they've crossed the border, it's not very well defined."

"But good God, they *must* know! Once they get out of the Madar Pass, they're in the Ogaden, we simply can't allow it!"

They were moving steadily down the hill, beating their gas cans; the din was appalling. I had never seen Sir Reginald so upset, and I said: "Yes, it could be awkward, couldn't it?"

"Awkward? Have you no sense at all? It's a deliberate affront!" I was almost waiting for him to say: "This could mean war, Commissioner."

I said instead: "Or would you rather go and deal with them yourself? A talk, perhaps . . ."

"*Talk* to them?" He was horrified. "I mustn't even *see* them! I'd have to make a formal protest to Addis Ababa, and London would be very difficult about it."

"Well, shall I go? That wouldn't be quite so official."

He looked at me for a moment as though he were wondering if I could handle it.

I said gently: "I'll take Tafeta with me, there'll be no trouble."

He thought for a while, and then: "Would you consider going without Tafeta?"

"Yes, of course."

Tafeta was nodding his head. He said: "Yes, it would be much better if you were alone. There'll be no trouble." He was peering across the space that separated us, his desert eyes marvelous. He seemed more amused than anything else, and he said: "The man on horseback, his name is Ras Michael, he comes from the Lake Hardameia area, a local chief."

"A bandit?"

"No, sir. He's a friend of His Majesty the Emperor."

"Lake Hardameia? Where is that exactly?"

"About thirty miles beyond the Madar Pass. But I didn't think he had so many soldiers."

"So he really is a bandit?"

"No, sir, definitely not. He claims a certain degree of autonomy, of course, like all the other chiefs. But a good man, I'd say. A little bit impetuous." He turned to Sir Reginald:

"If you'd care to return to Jig-Jigga, sir?"

The Governor was still in shock. He couldn't take his eyes off the approaching men, and he kept muttering: "I mustn't even see them . . . What the devil are they up to? An *army*, in *our* territory, I never heard of anything like it. . . ."

Suddenly aware that Tafeta had spoken to him, he said: "How's that?"

"You might prefer to leave the area, sir, until it's been taken care of?"

"Yes, yes, I think you're right, we really must avoid a confrontation. I think if you and I return to the truck . . . How far is that?"

It had been parked in the shade down in the valley, well out of sight and out of their path.

I said: "A couple of miles at most."

He nodded. "All right. Are you sure you can handle it? On a *personal* level?"

"I'm sure of it."

"You must get them out of this territory immediately."

I said: "All five hundred of them?"

But he was in no mood for sarcasm. He turned away and started walking quickly down the hill to the valley where the truck was parked. Tafeta smiled and said: "No trouble, I know it," and then followed him.

I noticed that the Somalis had all gone. They, too, were making tracks for the town, well scattered, and moving fast.

I waited a reasonable time, standing there in the evening sun and watching the line of soldiers get closer and closer, and when they were well within range, I hollered and waved my arm, and started walking toward them.

The horseman was coming in now, galloping hard, and he reined in tight and pranced his fine stallion right under my nose, and I was glad to see that he was laughing.

I held out my hand and said: "Ras Michael, isn't it?"

His English was excellent, and he reached down and shook hands and said: "Yes, you know me?"

"I know about you. I'm the Police Commissioner in this area."

"Yes, I know. And that was the Governor with you. Where did he get to?"

"He didn't want to see you, you're not supposed to be here. What goes on?"

He jumped off his horse and handed me his old army water bottle. It was full of *tej*. He said: "It's thirsty work. You know about the lions, of course. I hear you've been having trouble too."

"Yes, I know about them. We've been hunting them for a week."

"Oh? Any luck?"

"Nothing."

"You know about the big one? The one with the silver chain round its neck?"

"Silver chain?" It was the first I'd heard of it in this particular context, though there are always stories floating around of lions with silver chains, it's part of Africa's heritage.

He saw my puzzlement, and laughed and said: "No, I don't really believe it either. But they say one of them is a tame lion that used to belong to the Emperor. Marshal Graziani stole it from him and brought it down here to Jig-Jigga, and when the Italians got chased out, the lion went wild and escaped back into the bush. That's the story, anyway."

"Graziani was six or seven years ago, the time checks out all right. The experts tell me the leader of the pride is about ten years old."

"Well, it could be. But if it's the Emperor's old pet, we don't want it shot. So we've been driving them south, out of our territory."

I said: "Into ours."

He shrugged. "Well, who knows where the borders are?"

"The hill is the border, you're ten miles over it."

"Is that what the Governor's angry about?"

"Not so much angry, as shocked. Protocol, all that sort of thing. I'm sure you understand."

"Well, don't worry, we'll be on our way."

"Back to Lake Hardameia?"

"No. East."

"Then for another hundred and fifty miles you'll still be in our territory. After that, you're in British Somaliland."

"It's all the Ogaden, it's empty, nobody except Somalis.

Besides, we'll be driving them out of your area, that should make you happy."

"Will you keep clear of Jig-Jigga?"

"Of course, we don't want any trouble. His Majesty would object, too, if we showed ourselves in the town too much."

"So can I tell the Governor you're on your way out?"

"Of course. We don't want to stay here, this place is only fit for Somalis. When we get it back, we'll do something with it, chase all the Somalis over the border into Kenya. But for the moment, all we're chasing is lions."

He whistled to his stallion, and it came trotting over to him. He swung himself in the saddle, thrust out his hand, and said: "If you want to ride behind me, I'll take you into Jig-Jigga, save you a long walk."

I didn't know whether he was mocking me or not. He seemed a reasonable sort of man, with the careless scorn of authority—other than his own—which was typical of any local *Ras.* He was surprisingly young for an Amhara chief, not more than thirty or thirty-five years old. He wore a long, ornamental dagger in his belt, and an old Italian rifle was slung across his back, his chest crossed with leather bandoliers.

I could imagine the Governor's state of apoplexy if he should see me riding into town behind the *Ras,* so I shook my head and said: "No, I think I'd better go back alone, don't you? And thank you for the *tej,* it's very good."

"Would you like some more? Please." He held out the flask for me, and when I took it, he said: "Keep it, a souvenir. Ras Michael, I'm glad you know my name."

With a wave of the hand he was gone, riding fast up the hill to where the line was moving slowly forward.

I walked back down the hill, into the little green valley, and found the Governor waiting in the small copse where the truck was parked. I told him the intruders were on their way out, and he looked pleased and wisely refrained from asking *when.*

We drove off slowly toward the town, and when the engine started boiling over we stopped by a small *rer* to ask for water.

We called out *"Hodi"* and waited, and were invited into the thorn enclosure where the water jars were stored, and the elderly Somali who lived there carefully measured some out for us into a can, and I noticed that a young girl, perhaps sixteen or seventeen years old, was sitting in a corner by herself, weeping, a piece of sacking over her head.

I said to the Somali, in Italian: *"Che c'e, what's the trouble with the woman?"*

He shrugged, quite unconcerned, and said: *"Mia moglie, my wife."*

He chose to continue in Somali, so he switched languages and turned to the Governor. There was a great deal of contempt in his manner, either for us, or for the girl who was unseemly enough to display her emotion over what he obviously regarded as a trivial matter.

Sir Reginald listened intently, looking at me from time to time, and at last he said: "The young girl is his latest wife, she had a baby a month ago, and last night the lions came and ate it."

"He doesn't seem to be very upset about it."

"No, he's not. When I offered my sympathy, he said it was a female child, so it doesn't matter very much. He has enough sons. It's just the mother who's upset."

I said: "And that's the eleventh, isn't it?"

"Just as the *fal* said. And the lions are being . . . asked to leave."

We carried the water back to the truck, filled up the radiator, and drove back into town.

We never saw the lions again.

14

It seemed strange to me that throughout the whole of our territory—as, indeed, throughout most of Africa—the varied ethnic groups always seemed to band together, seeking the comfort of mutual language or custom, and somehow maintaining a characteristic way of life in a world that was not always acceptable to them.

It was understandable that the Somalis and the Ethiopians should live apart from each other and mingle as little as possible; each disliked the other so virulently that no alternative was possible. Overtly, they were correct and formal with each other when circumstances forced them to mingle—the Ethiopians proud, the Somalis haughty—but a long history of Christian-Moslem warfare had left a simmering, mutual hatred that seemed always ready to boil over.

The Ethiopians had been converted to Christianity in the fourth century by the Phoenician Frumentius, who was sailing down the Red Sea and looking for India, and who subsequently became installed in Axum as the first Bishop of Abyssinia under the name of Abba Salama, or Father of Peace. And ever since then, the strange spectacle of a Christian Kingdom, and a semi-barbaric one at that, in the very heart of a pagan world, had been anathema to the warlike peoples who crowded her borders on all sides. "An island of Christians in a sea of Pagans," said the Emperor Menelik, and it is worth noting that within two hundred years they had pushed the shores of that island as far east as Arabia itself. But for their defeat before the walls of Mecca in A.D. 570—the probable year of the Prophet Mohammed's birth—it is at least likely that the Islamic revolution, which changed the state of the world, would have been stifled at its inception. They were driven, then, out of Asia, and went back to their mountains in Tigre, and from that time on, cut off from the rest of the Christian world, they held stoutly to their religion and fought off the Moslem hordes who were sweeping through Africa.

And now, those Moslems, the Somalis, were among them. Arbitration had taken the place of the sword, and a foreign power was stationed on their soil to keep the peace. But that peace was very fragile.

And so, they kept to themselves, each side wary of the other. It was understandable, and perhaps even necessary.

But the same segregation, instinctive and somewhat chauvinistic, was common, too, among the Europeans who lived in the territories, those who had chosen, for one reason or another, the exclusive life of the exile.

There were many of them.

The Italians, banding together in the early days because of their fear of retribution from the Ethiopians, were still, after all these years, living in a world that was entirely their own.

They gathered together in the cafés and the workshops, and in the course of time quite took them over, so that what was once Ethiopian or Somali took on a strong Napolitan, or Piedmontese, or Venetian atmosphere. The pungent scent of Africa was washed away in homemade red wine, and the dreary sounds of interminable Somali arguments about camels gave way to the fine, strident voices of truck drivers at lusty work on *"Santa Lucia"* or *"O sole mio"* . . . (The Italians tended to migrate toward the Somali quarters; they feared them less than the Ethiopians.) Their girls, young, cheerful, and loving, hung around them unabashed and carefree, dressed in European style with bright colors and an unstudied elegance that was quite charming.

Wherever there was machinery, or a kitchen, you would find the Italians clustered together, and each one of them seemed to carry, permanently, a wrench in one hand, and a can of their ubiquitous tomato paste in the other. They built the roads, they kept the trucks going, and that fine Italianate art of survival, of making do under adverse circumstances, kept their colony flourishing. They lived *andante e con brio*, carrying Italy on their shoulders wherever they went, and you were always very much aware of their presence. If you came across one of their convoys in the bush, you could smell the rich, ripe bolognese sauce of their dinners even before you were aware of the stench of Diesel oil.

The Greeks, on the other hand, were much less intrusive. They always seemed to live in small dark houses where little light came in, as though they were constantly in hiding. There would always be piles of hard goatskins outside their doors, or boxes of incense, or heavy sacks of coffee. There would always be a curtain hanging over the kitchen entrance, behind which an outsized woman in bare feet was always cooking something, and you never knew if she was the wife, the mother, or the mistress, because she always looked ageless and sullen and had nothing whatever to say; she was never introduced to visitors.

The Greeks were the traders, and the men with the money, though they never liked to display their wealth. They owned the hotels and the banks, invariably, and at night they would come out of their dark houses, carefully but conservatively dressed in gray suits—a little shabby, not to make the wrong impression—with white shirts carefully ironed by the woman back there, and they would sit in the cafés to play poker; they were murder with a pack of cards. Night after night, hotels, stores, even banks would change hands at the poker table. They always knew what was for sale, how much they would have to pay for it, and where they could sell it again at a profit. And they were generous in the extreme.

We were playing one night, some of the police with a few of the railway officials, when Liveratos, the Greek who ran the coffee industry, came and joined us. The stakes got too high for my blood, and I pulled out, and I saw Liveratos lose, with a full house in his hand, to Harry Blake—with three jacks. I asked him about it later, and the Greek merely shrugged and said: "Nearly a hundred pounds on the table. I don't need it. Harry Blake does, he's got troubles on his hands." I never did find out what the trouble was; but it seems that Harry solved it with his unexpected winnings.

They dealt, and double-dealt, with each other, and the accumulation of wealth was their sole raison d'être. They were well enough liked, on the whole; only everyone thought they were a little furtive.

The French were more gregarious. They too tended to become traders, but they dealt, it always seemed, in the luxuries. The free port of Djibouti, more French than Paris, was within quick and easy reach, so they kept the territory supplied with vintage wines, and good cognacs, with perfumes, and all the canned delicacies, the *pâtés* and *fromages,* which sometimes made us wonder if we were still in Africa. They mixed easily

197

with everybody, but only superficially; it never seemed possible to get close to them. They were great smugglers, working very discreetly because they were never quite sure how the law stood, and they sat smiling in their cafés while underlings delivered cases of produce to their cellars, not secretly, but not very openly either.

The Poles and the Czechs lived in hotels, always, and I could never discover just why; perhaps the impermanence that recent history had imposed on their homelands was part of the reason, though they would never admit this. They surrounded themselves with the absolute minimum of personal paraphernalia, and were always distrusted, very slightly, by the Ethiopians. Even Count Vilaski, the Polish aristocrat with his opaque monocle, was regarded with a great deal of suspicion; everyone was sure that he was an agent for Moscow, a fiction he took great delight in encouraging, though it was not true. He had lost an eye fighting the Russians in Warsaw, and had lost all his family too. He had simply gathered together what funds he could lay his hands on, and had chosen Ethiopia as his new home, merely because, he claimed, the whole of Europe was in the hands of upstarts, and Ethiopia was the only truly feudal country left in the world. He did not work, and was fond of announcing that when his money ran out, as it undoubtedly would one day, he would simply kill himself. I always believed that he spoke the truth.

The Armenians . . . these strange people were always a race apart. Nobody seems to know anything about the Armenians, except that they were all once massacred on the slopes of Musa Dagh. There were no more than a dozen of them in the territories, and without exception they were secretive, devious, and of remarkably high intelligence; they all seemed to have their native flair for knowing exactly what was happening around them. They always seemed to speak wonderfully fluent English, and Amharic, and Somali, and French, and Italian, and any other language that would help them along. They mixed, on equal but slightly hesitant terms, with everyone, from the Governor to the street sweepers, and they seemed to have a penchant for living a little way from everyone else, on the outskirts of the towns, in rustic little houses with savage wild dogs around them. Like the Greeks, they lived well and made money. Like the French, they got along easily with everyone and caused no trouble. And like the Italians, they were ready to flee at the first sign of danger.

These were the people that gave the "European" parts of the Territories their own particular charm. The term "melting-pot" comes to mind except that they were never fused into one coherent whole; and it was this natural segregation that brought to the Territory its varied excitements.

Why were they here? The lovely little towns of Africa are always filled with exiles; no one ever knows just where they come from, or where they are going. I was one of them myself, and enjoying it just as much as the rest of them.

* * *

I had been going over the police budget that day, and had found that my gardener, an unobtrusive and friendly old man who pottered around the grounds of the house all day and slept in the kitchen somewhere, was not on the payroll.

I sent for Superintendent Aklilu, who had prepared the figures, and told him of the omission. He seemed surprised.

He said: "Oh, no, the gardener's not paid. He's a slave. You must have seen the marks on his forehead." There were two tiny burns at his temples, a permanent indication of his status.

I said: "My God, you're not telling me I keep a slave?"

"Yes, sir. It's perfectly all right, he never has been paid, all his life. He doesn't even expect it."

"Jesus."

I'm not particularly inhibited, but I wondered what London would say if I were to add to the Budget Commentary: "plus one slave, working as a gardener to the Commissioner of Police."

I said to the Superintendent: "I think you'd better get him over here right away, we'll straighten this out *now.*"

The gardener's name was Damtu, and he was probably about fifty years old. He cut the grass, and kept the house supplied with whatever flowers there were, and gathered the tomatoes, and dozed a great deal during the heat of the day under the huge *kosso* tree, its branches laden with pendant red flowers that shaded the veranda. He was an Arussi from the southern lowlands, and spoke only his native dialect and a very limited amount of Amharic, so we had no common language. We would chat together once in a while, nonetheless; he spoke Arussi, I spoke Italian, and each hoped that some of it, with gestures, was getting through. He would greet me cheerfully when I came home from work, and made a point of always opening the gate for me, a broad smile on his face when I left for my HQ in the mornings. He wore my cast-off clothing (as an Arussi, he would normally wear only skins), and ate from the household supplies. Somehow, it seemed that he was always just there, cheerful and friendly and perfectly content.

He came to the office now, looking a little nervous; it was the first time he had ever been there. With Aklilu interpreting, I said carefully: "I understand, Damtu, that all the time I've been here you've never been paid a salary."

He was frowning, unsure of himself. He nodded. "Of course not. I'm a slave, I always have been, since I was a boy."

I said: "Well, you're not any more. You're on the payroll now, and we'll arrange for back pay, at least from the time of our administration."

He did not seem to understand. Aklilu was showing very marked signs of disapproval as he translated, and I was prepared to be very firm about it. They argued for a while, and then, to my astonishment, I saw that the old man was crying. Aklilu turned to me, very reproachfully, and said: "I'm afraid you've hurt him terribly. You've really upset him."

I couldn't believe it. I had thought that the tears were an expression of a quite different emotion. I told Aklilu that I didn't understand what he meant, and he said, very patiently: "He wants to know if that's all he means to you. He thought that the relationship was better than a merely financial one."

"But for God's sake, he's got to be paid for his work!"

"No, he doesn't think so. He doesn't want to be reduced to the level of a mere servant."

It was quite incomprehensible; I was the uncomprehending alien again, unable to assimilate the finer points of a local philosophy. I felt I was imposing my own way of life on someone who, quite tacitly, didn't really like it very much.

I said: "But tell him, he'd be a comparatively rich man with all that back pay."

Aklilu nodded. "Of course. But don't you see . . . For forty years or more, he's been fed, and clothed, and housed, and someone has always told him what to do. . . . He's never had to make a decision in his life. He wouldn't know what to do with money."

"But he *can't* be satisfied with that."

"But he *is.*" There was a little silence. Damtu was unashamedly weeping, the tears rolling down his face. Aklilu said, at last, talking like a tutor with a rather dull child: "It's a question of his personal dignity. By offering him money, you've put a price on his work, and he thinks that's a terribly cruel thing to do."

I said, protesting: "But he'd still have the food, the clothing, the housing . . ." It didn't seem much for an honest man's labor. "He could use the money to buy himself a wife, or . . . or any of the things he's always wanted. Tell him that I'm grateful for the work he does for me, and that I'd like to pay him for it."

The silence was longer now. And then Aklilu said, diffidently: "Of course, *Commandante*, if you insist, I will. But really, I'd much rather not. I'm afraid you've already hurt his feelings quite considerably. It would be very much better to say that it was all a mistake."

Inspector Gabre had come into the office, on another matter, and was nodding his head, agreeing. I looked at the three of them, frustrated again, and said: "And apologize to him?"

Aklilu nodded. "Yes, that would help, certainly."

I felt that he was very angry about the whole thing, glad to find a way out. And I must confess, the more I thought about it, the more easily I could understand Damtu's reasoning; the urgent need for money is not universally shared.

So I explained, rather lamely perhaps, that my own foreign philosophies had prompted a mistake, which I regretted. I told Damtu I would not interfere with his status, if he were sure he was satisfied with it.

He was sure. He looked at me a little dubiously as Aklilu translated, as though he were not convinced he'd ever be able to trust me again. Watching him, it seemed to me that I had unwittingly shattered a little dream; a tragic one, but a dream nonetheless. It's often with the best intentions that we make the worst mistakes.

Damtu went back to work, and to this day, I imagine, he's still dozing contentedly, through the heat of the day, under that beautiful *kosso* tree.

For a few days, things were never quite the same between us. But quite soon, the wound healed.

* * *

It was time for a visit to Jig-Jigga again. Sir Reginald had sent me an urgent summons which had taken three days to reach me; the telephones weren't working.

The Governor had been down there, among his beloved Somalis, for more than a week now. Once in a while, he liked to escape from what he thought of as the excessive sophistication of Dire-Daua, and feel the raw sand under his feet again. He liked to be greeted in the marketplace not with the respect that his position entitled him to, but with the casual, one-of-us friendliness given to a man who has spent almost his entire life among the simple tribesmen of the villages.

The great market here was the center of the Somali culture, and the crowds here came from all the tribes and subtribes that wandered over the empty, hostile desert, driving their camels with them in the unending search for water. Sometimes, they came to buy or sell their stock, to trade for woolen cloth, or rope, or water *jaras*, or copper and brass ornaments for their women. Sometimes, they came to stay, the young ones, deserting the rigors of their tribal life for the ease and noisy pleasures of the town.

It is part of the pattern, of course, all over Africa—the slow but inexorable breakup of the old traditions of the bush, and the encroachment on them of the settled form of existence of which the town is the symbol. For the young men, the town was a challenge, a chance to meet, and to argue with others from outside their own family unit, and to hatch their constant plots, one against the other, on a larger scale than they had known before; and here too, the tribes kept to their own enclaves, distrusting their neighbors and always ready to litigate with them.

For the young women, there was a different lure.

The dowry is still part of the marriage system among the Somalis, and payment is customarily made with camels. But among the poorer families (and wealth is measured by the size of the herd), even three or four camels, the dowry for a young girl's marriage, was an insupportable expense. And frequently, very frequently, these outlying villagers would send their daughters in to Jig-Jigga to work in the town's brothels for a year or two to acquire the necessary wealth.

As in the West, there was always a certain social stigma attached to prostitution, but here it was on a very much lesser scale, so slight, on occasion, as to be of no worth at all; it was accepted as a fact of life—and a necessary one at that.

There had always been prostitutes in Jig-Jigga, as far back as anyone could remember, but in the days of the Italian occupation, its quality, as well as its quantity, had been considerably augmented. The military brothel was part of the Italian army life, and before our arrival it had taken on a certain nonchalant order, quite unregulated in any way, but settling down into a definite pattern.

The Street of the Brothels itself was just an ordinary dirt-paved street, between dusty, whitewashed, one-story houses, with ragged children playing in the street and goats and chickens wandering about. Sometimes, a plump and cheerful madam would be sitting barefoot on a wooden chair outside her house, taking in the sun and watching the passersby, or sometimes a pretty young Galla girl would be lounging in her doorway, dressed in a bright cotton print that someone had brought her from Mogadiscio or Dire-Daua or Djibouti, but there was never much of an overt indication that this street was different from any of the others. And the girls, for the most part extremely young, came from all the scattered camps that lay among the sandy folds of the desert to the east, or from the little villages that dotted the green hills to the west.

Sitting around Armetta's restaurant for most of their time, adding their bright colors and inconsequential chatter to the general chaos, they seemed happy; they came and went, like the population of the town, so that the faces were constantly changing. They would work for a year or two, and then go back to their homes, and sooner or later get married.

But here, as in all Moslem countries, the tradition of chastity in a bride is held in considerable merit, and to this end, a peculiar form of female circumcision is practiced almost universally among them. It is customary for a young girl's vagina to be sealed by stitching when she reaches puberty, and for the seal to be broken surgically when she marries.

It is a simple, though probably extremely painful, operation. The inner surface of the two *labia majore* are slit with a knife, the two edges pulled together and sutured with needle and thread, or a thin piece of wire, or (among the desert tribes) with cactus thorns. In the course of a few weeks, the vaginal opening is completely closed, and the girl's continued virginity is assured until the time when, at her marriage, it is once more opened with the point of a dagger. The ritual reopening is done by the bride's mother, sometimes by the husband himself. A handful of wood ash is rubbed into the wound as a disinfectant and coagulate, and the girl is immediately ready for copulation.

The young girls came into the town, here, by the hundreds. They would voluntarily submit to the slicing open of the sealed vagina, go to work as prostitutes for a year or so, and then have the opening stitched up a second time to permit access to their husbands, once more, as virgins; but relatively wealthy ones.

The girls came, and conquered, and went; and new ones took their places.

The Lancia broke down that day, in the middle of the Madar Pass, and the driver, his immaculate uniform spotted with blood which he had coughed up (it was the day of his operation), ran the twelve miles to the town to get help. And a few hours later, Lucertola arrived with a truck to tow me in, a rather undignified entrance for a Police Commissioner.

The Governor, somewhat to my surprise—the urgency of his

message had worried me a little—was in a very genial mood. He said, pouring a Black Velvet: "The doctor here tells me that the incidence of venereal disease in Jig-Jigga is nearly fifty percent. Can you believe it? Nearly fifty percent!"

I said: "First of all, he can't possibly be sure of that. And secondly, it's not really very high. In Siwa, it's one hundred percent."

"Siwa?" He blinked. "And you can't be sure of that either, can you? Do you know how many prostitutes there are in town at this moment? He tells me the figure is nearly two thousand. I think we should do something about it."

"Oh? What did you have in mind?"

Armina was hovering, wishing she spoke better English. She gestured broadly and said: "*Due mille butane, e troppo,*" and I knew that she was up to one of her schemes again.

The Governor blinked at me again and said: "Well, I thought we ought to weed out the sick ones and send them back to their villages, what do you think?"

"Leaving only the clean ones behind to get infected by the men, is that the idea?"

"Well . . . Then what do you suggest?"

"I suggest we do nothing. Nothing at all. Or we could move them around a bit and have a VD side of the street and a clean side of the street. Higher prices for quality, like the milk without the sand in it."

"Well, if you want to be flippant about it . . ."

I said: "Reggie, we can't deport one thousand women all of a sudden, even if we had the authority to do it, which I doubt."

"No, I suppose it might be a little difficult."

He got up and began pacing up and down, throwing a glance at Armina once in a while. Her face was blank and expressionless, but I had the feeling that she wanted to urge him on and didn't quite know how to do it unobtrusively. She said something to him in Somali, very quietly, and he shook his head, irritated. I wondered what it was he really wanted to see me about.

He said at last: "I've come to the conclusion that there are elements in the police administration here that are not as . . . as "clean" as they should be. There's something going on that I don't like at all, not a bit. There's . . . there's *dishonesty.*"

There is nothing in the world worse than a corrupt policeman, and there will always be the bad apple in the barrel. I had thought that we were fairly good down here, in this respect. But it was his use of the word "administration" that worried me; it indicated something rather more than a cop on the beat shaking down a resident or two. I waited, and he said at last, taking a deep breath: "Someone in your office is accepting bribes."

He was terribly nervous. There was an air about him of having been pushed into saying something he really wanted to know nothing of; it disturbed me deeply.

I said: "I'm very surprised. In *my* office? I think I'd have heard about it, one way or another. Do you know who it is?"

"No. I don't."

"And what's the source of your information?"

He waved a vague hand in the air. "It's common knowledge. Somebody is selling visas to the Somalis who want to cross the border. They're supposed to be free, you know that."

"Of course I know it. And they *are* free."

"Well, someone's accepting money for them."

Armina was very quiet, watching us.

I said: "And you don't know who it is? None of your Somali friends has even mentioned a name?"

"No."

I knew it was a lie, and knew that he was going to be damned adamant about it, so I told him I'd look into it and left it at that. I had a very uncomfortable feeling that something had come between us, that he was forcing himself to be both patient and friendly when, at that moment, he was very upset indeed about me personally. There was a feeling of separation among us, as though we were all, for the moment, in three individual camps. I wondered if he'd push it any harder, but he seemed relieved that it was over. Armina said brightly, very suddenly: "I'm sure it's nothing to worry about. Why don't I make you some coffee? Would you like that?"

I nodded, and she went into the kitchen, and the Governor said, whispering, smiling hesitantly: "I'm sure it's going to be all right, really." I thought I had never seen a man so acutely uncomfortable.

I changed the subject abruptly, and said: "I borrowed Lucertola to work on the Lancia, is that all right?"

He brightened at once, a difficult subject thrust behind him, and said: "Yes, of course, he really is an awfully good mechanic. Did you find out what it was?"

"The petrol pump is broken."

"Well, he'll take care of it."

We chatted over our coffee for a while, and when I walked back to my office, Lucertola had stripped down the pump and was fitting a new washer to it. He looked at me sideways, and thought for a moment, and then said: "Well, they didn't fire you, I hope?"

I felt suddenly very angry with him. I said: "No, why the hell should they?"

He was smiling, looking rather conspiratorial, as though he knew all the answers. He said carefully: "I think you should know, *Commandante*, there's a story going round. *C'e una storia, una storia . . .*"

"This is a very provincial town, Lucertola. There's always gossip going around, we don't have to pay too much attention to it."

He was quiet for a little while, but I could see that he was aching to tell me something, and finally I asked him what it was all about.

He said, fiddling with his wrench: "It's not very pleasant. But Armina told the Governor that you were taking bribes from the Somalis. Something to do with travel permits for over the border."

"So it's Armina again."

"*Quella vacca,* Armina."

"And how did you find out about it?"

He shrugged: "There's not much in that house that's secret. She talks with the servants, they talk with me. Bazaar gossip."

"And do you know why she's telling him that?"

"It's obvious. The affair of the bank robbery. You know the Somalis, she'll never forgive you for that."

"I see. But I don't think for one minute that he believes her."

He was very serious all of a sudden. He said, frowning: "He believes everything she tells him. Everything. *E furba, quella donna,* she's a very crafty woman. You get into her bad books, *Commandante,* there'll be nothing but trouble." He shrugged broadly. "And that's where you are, in her bad books. She's afraid you'll tell him the real story behind the bank robbery. She wants to get her say in first."

"The real story? I wish we knew it."

He nodded, smiling secretively. I always had the impression that he had something up his sleeve. He said: "The Somalis, I know them well. And I know that cow better than anyone."

I felt the whole thing was extremely distasteful. I said: "Well, fix that bloody pump, Lucertola, and mind your own bloody business. Just forget about it."

"Yes, sir."

209

That's what I did too. I forgot about the whole thing, and let it die a natural death. The Governor never mentioned it again, and Armina and I remained the best of friends. At least, on the surface.

15

My wife arrived at last, and even here, the circumstances were remarkable.

She was in London, trying to cope with the immediate chaos of postwar organization and find a flight that would bring her out here; and her long letters told me of the frustration that the civilian population was suffering from. The ships, the planes were all now feeling the effects of six years of war and depletion; and as far as the War Office was concerned, there was just no way to send wives out to Africa to join their husbands.

She pulled a few strings, spoke with a few friends, hitchhiked a little and cut a few corners, and finally found her way to Ethiopia under her own steam, which, at times, is considerable. By ship, plane, bus, river steamer, and broken-down truck; over deserts, through forests, and across swamps; a series of remarkable adventures attesting to her determination, she finally—just turned up. Her last letter to me, which arrived coincidentally with her body, had stated: "There is absolutely no hope of finding any transport in the foreseeable future, you'll probably never see me again."

And then, one evening, coming back to my house after a lazy day at the office, I found a young Somali waiting for me. He wanted a job as a servant. I told him I was already well taken care of, that I was living alone, and could manage very well as things were. I even offered to send him to one of the other exiles who might have hired him, but he said, smiling: "When the lady gets here, you will need another man in the house."

I wondered how he knew that her coming here, sooner or later, was even contemplated, but I merely said: "She won't be out here for a long, long time," and he beamed happily and said: "No. She's on her way now."

I said: "Oh? And what makes you think that?"

He shrugged: "A *fal* told me."

It seemed unlikely that a Somali witch doctor would know anything about the intricacies of military movement orders, so I shrugged it off and sent him on his way. But I reflected for a while on the inexplicable workings of the Somali mind, and that evening, at Reggie's house, I said to him: "One of your Somalis tells me Aliza is on her way here."

He shook his head, smiling gently. "No, I think not. I would have heard about it."

"He was told by a *fal* that she'd be here in a day or two."

"A *fal*?" He was startled. "Oh dear. Then perhaps I'd better check. Although the last telegram said, what was it? that she couldn't possibly get here for several months." He spoke to Armina for a while, and she nodded wisely and beamed at me, and he said at last: "Yes, I think I'd better ask London about it again."

"Can you do that?"

"Of course. I'll send a cable off first thing in the morning."

"I can't believe a young man fresh in from the desert knows more than we do."

He smiled easily: "Let's find out, shall we?"

The next morning, the cable duly went off, and the answer came back in a few hours. It was to the effect that the delay was regretted, but my wife was still in London waiting for a ship to take her, first to Alexandria, and then on to Ethiopia; with luck, I could expect her in a matter of six or seven weeks.

At that time, she was in Cairo.

And three days later, I got a signal from Hargeisa, over the border in British Somaliland; she was there, waiting for a truck to take her on her way, or would I come and fetch her?

There was a flurry of excitement everywhere. The Governor began to worry again about his illicit romance, but Armina smiled and said happily: "Eh, she's a woman, she'll understand." We polished up the house, and I borrowed the Governor's big Dodge because the Lancia had broken down again. And I set off, with Lucertola beside me to drive us back, up the steep, steep mountain to Harar, down through the red-sand mystery of the Madar Pass, and out across the empty desert that spread out below Jig-Jigga, and over the border.

* * *

It was in the middle of the afternoon when we hit the mountain road on the way home.

We sat in the back, my wife and I, holding hands and looking out over the purple mountains, as Lucertola, a highly skilled but somewhat reckless driver, pushed the wartime car at high speed along the twisting, dangerous bends. I checked him once for speeding, I remember, but the road, as usual, was

213

empty, and we were sweeping round the hairpins at better than fifty miles an hour, trying to get back before sundown.

And then, it happened.

We came round one of the bends, very fast, with the high granite cliff close beside us on one side and a drop of a thousand feet or more on the other, and an ancient truck was coming toward us, dead center in the road, with maybe five or six feet on either side of it. I felt the brakes go on hard, but the car was old and a little decrepit, and it slewed over to one side, the beginnings of a bad skid that could take us over the edge.

I grabbed the squab of the front seat and watched, and in the split second of acute danger I knew that there was only one thing to be done—a highly complicated maneuver that would ram our right-side front wheel, at speed, under the truck's right-side rear wheel, and wedge us safely in position. It was one of those cases where you know exactly what has to be done, the only thing to be done; and are equally sure that the driver's got another idea that's not going to work.

But that, indeed, is what Lucertola did. For one frantic moment, we headed for the great abyss, and then he wrenched the wheel hard over, a jagged, grinding sound, and rammed us under the truck's body.

Both our left-side wheels were over the edge, spinning crazily. But we were firmly locked in position, the radiator spouting boiling water, and the right-side front crumpled into a mess. The right-side doors were jammed shut; and when we threw open the rear left, the bottom of the gorge, a sheet drop, was eight, nine hundred feet or more below us.

My wife was trembling. Lucertola and I clambered out, very gingerly, and hauled her, squealing a trifle, up and over the car's shattered body to safety.

The driver of the truck, an ancient Amhara, was quite unhurt, and was roaring with laughter at the calamity; he would have something to talk about for years.

We backed his vehicle, locked tightly to ours, slowly down the hill a little till all our wheels were on firm ground, and we exchanged polite remarks about each other's competence with a steering wheel for a while, and then we manhandled the two of them apart, crowbarred the front fenders out of the way of our wheels, and then coasted slowly down the hill to Dire-Daua.

The Governor was aghast at the wreck we had made of his car. He said suspiciously: "Are you sure Lucertola was driving?"

I said: "I was in the back with my wife, it's been a long time. And if I'd have been driving, it wouldn't have happened."

"Uh-huh." He recovered quickly and greeted my wife with great affection (they subsequently became very good friends), and even Armina showed no signs of the sullen anger she must have felt. Her own position was diminished, just slightly; she had always considered herself as the territory's First Lady, even if she had to hide in the kitchen when visiting generals from across the border came calling; and now, she could no longer quite get away with that thought. But her attitude was correct, courteous, and even affable.

But you could never tell what was going on in her mind.

* * *

We made an inspection, together, of the limitless deserts I was supposed to be watching over, driving an ancient, wartime ten-tonner, with a truckload of police, as bodyguards, following along behind. We camped out in the bush at night, and slept beside fires of thorn twigs, and lived on venison steaks and partridge soup and ostrich-egg omelettes.

(The ostrich egg is a very useful article of diet in the bush. Its shell is hard as iron; you bore a hole in with the point of your knife, thrust in a stick to stir up the contents, and pour as much as you need into the hot skillet, then seal up the hole

215

with a stopper of rag, or paper, or cork, and toss it into the back of the truck for the next time.)

We explored the lovely Madar, and watched the red brown hyrax scuttling in their ochre caves, and the idiot guinea fowl strutting among the rocks, and the tiny mouse deer streaking across the sand. We crisscrossed the plain in our own personal column of fine red dust that went with us everywhere, and we caught a couple of baby ostriches for pets, bright and inquisitive and delightful, though they soon lose, it seems, their baby intelligence and turn into nincompoops.

We found some hot sulfur springs to lie in under the sun, and emerged from them covered with a dry, yellow paste that cured every scar and cut on our bodies—the safari trademarks —and left our skins as smooth as a baby's behind. We bartered in the villages for beadwork, and drank camels' milk in the camps, and, in short, behaved like tourists on holiday, with very little thought of police duties that had never seemed very pressing anyway. We slept under the bright moon, and awoke when the sun hit our faces.

We spent one night in the bush as far north as the territory went, close by the borders of the Galla country, and in the early hours of the morning, the darkness acute, I felt a light touch on my shoulder. It was our Somali Sergeant.

He whispered: *"Absi, danger."*

The camp fires were low, and I thought at first he was worried about lion, and I said: *"Libah?"*

He shook his head and pointed: *"Shifta."*

The word *shifta* means, literally, bandits, and refers as a rule to any group of Somalis who have forsaken their kraal—usually when the water dries up—and have not been able to find any new territory they can claim as their own. When this happens, they take to their spears and an occasional rifle, and wander around the deserts preying on other nomads, or on any truck convoys that might be passing through. To their own natural hostility to the rest of the world at large, they have added the menace of lawlessness, and they will murder for as little as a piece of rag, an empty can to carry milk in, or a skin to fashion into sandals. The man who has nothing will kill for very little, and in his own empty world it is hard to blame him for it.

Among the ten men of our bodyguard, there were three Ethiopians, and I saw that they had silently taken up positions very close to the two of us, their rifles ready in the darkness. One of them was gently pushing sand over the fire's embers, darkening them. The rest of them had moved farther out, making a ring around our tiny camp, and I woke my wife and put her aboard the truck with Tadessa, our personal servant, who was an Amhara, a tall, tough young man of twenty years or so who was always ready to take on the whole Somali nation and tear it apart with his strong teeth. He said, not deigning to whisper: "Give me your rifle, *signore*, I will kill them all."

We gathered our forces together in the silence and waited.

I said: "How many of them, do you know?" I could see nothing.

The Sergeant pointed again: "There, by the bushes, three of them. Three or four more over there, about ten of them a little farther away, and six or seven more behind us. As far as I can see, about twenty-five of them. Perhaps a lot more."

They were waiting out there in the night, not moving.

I said: "If they have rifles . . ."

He nodded. "They would have used them by now."

"So we sit up the rest of the night, and wait."

He said, hesitantly: "I can talk with them if you wish."

"All right."

He stood up and shouted, and waited, and shouted again, and then again, and at last, out of the blackness and the silence, the disembodied voice came back. It was taken up on one side, and on the other, and finally behind us; they wanted us to understand that they were all around us. And at last, the

Sergeant said: "They want our rifles. They say if we give them the guns, they will let us go on our way in peace."

"Tell them to go to hell."

"Yes, sir."

He shouted at them again, and then there was silence, and for the rest of the night we just sat there, thinking that as a major encounter it was all a bit of a farce. And when at last the sun came up, the desert was as empty as it had ever been.

They had gone.

The horizon was bleak and lifeless and arid, bright gold under the morning sun, and the poor wandering nomads were already far beyond it. We decided we would spend the final night of our safari in Jig-Jigga, where the excitements were of a vastly different kind. We drove off slowly, bumping over the desert. In the back of the truck, Satan, the cheetah, was growling over a leg of venison.

Our house, there, was one of three that had been put up by the Italians in the time of their occupation, and it stood just across the road from the village, the dirt road that ran from the Madar Pass to the border and Hargeisa. It was comfortable enough, a little oversimple as houses go, with a single bedroom, a large living room with double front doors of teak leading directly into it, a bathroom of sorts (the water was heated by a charcoal fire under an old oil drum of water that stood on the outisde of the bathroom wall; the hot water merely ran down, by gravity, into the bath as soon as the plug in the drum was pulled out), and an outside kitchen and storeroom, where our two cows slept. (The milk had become sandier than ever, and I had solved the problem by buying a cow and a calf.)

There was a pleasant little garden, mostly devoted to rampant tomatoes, self-seeded everywhere, with a few zinnias and periwinkle for color and not much else except sand.

It was one of the Ethiopians' countless holidays, a saint's day, and in honor of the occasion I had presented the police barracks with an ox, which would be slaughtered that night and eaten raw at their celebration. I had been invited to attend, but had refused, on the grounds that my august presence might have inhibited their enjoyments; I was quite wrong about that, as it turned out.

A young English girl had turned up unexpectedly, the wife of a soldier in Hargeisa whom my wife had met on the journey out. Her name was Dorothy, a bright and cheerful young woman on her first trip out from England, and she had come to spend a few days with us while her husband was fixing his house back there. And as we sat together in the living room late that night, we heard a strange, rumbling, chanting sort of sound, coming to us from the direction of the village, and when I stood at the open doorway looking out, I saw a huge column of men approaching, more than a hundred of them, carrying flares and jumping up and down as they moved toward us.

Tadessa was suddenly there, looking a little anxious and saying authoritatively: "I think I'd better lock the doors."

He closed them and bolted them firmly, and it occurred to me that it is on such occasions as this that the exile feels, more acutely, his strangeness; I simply had no idea what was going on. I looked at Tadessa, who was scowling as though he wasn't very sure either, and he said: "I think they're coming here, and they're very drunk, *signore*. It would be better if we locked the ladies in the bedroom . . ."

The two girls didn't seem unduly worried (I found out later that they were both scared stiff), but it occurred to me that a couple of wooden doors would not present much of an obstacle to a small army of Ethiopians, drunk or sober. Nonetheless, Tadessa was a local man, and the locals always know best, so we put them in the bedroom and locked the door on them, and then the approaching column was trampling over the zinnias, and in no time at all the heavy front doors simply crashed off their hinges and flattened themselves on the ground. And more than a hundred policemen poured into the room, dancing and singing and sweating, stomping their great feet on the concrete floor and yelling at the tops of their voices.

One of them threw his arms around me and hugged me to his broad chest, a lion of a man in from the desert; he nearly squeezed the life out of me there and then. The chaos was indescribable, and I stood there like an idiot, not knowing what the hell it was all about. But Tadessa was suddenly very happy and he said, translating: "A party, *signore*, they want you to join them."

One of the men, a Sergeant, so drunk he could hardly stand up, raised his arms for silence, and made a flowery speech at me in Amharic, and I thanked him gravely, not knowing what he was talking about, and told Tadessa to break out the beer.

Fortunately, we kept rather large stocks of all the necessities, and there were more than a dozen cases of Addis Ababa beer in the storeroom. Three or four of the men lugged the heavy crates in, and prized off the tops with their teeth, and drank themselves silly. I noticed, admiringly, that some of the police from the outlying stations, who were really bushmen in uniform, found it just as easy to bite the tops off the bottles, spitting out the broken glass on the floor, under their bare feet. (They have a standard way of opening a can of corned beef, or of sardines—anything with a flange on it; you simply take the flange in your teeth, and turn the can against your chin. I tried it once; it's quite impossible.)

We drank together, all of us in the crowded room, for an hour. They never once attempted to get to the bedroom, and their behavior, though rowdy, was impeccable. At last, they picked me up on their shoulders and tossed me from one to another as we went out across the tomato plants to the street, over to Armetta's café for more beer and still more beer, then down the Street of the Brothels where we all drank still more. I have a hazy recollection of finishing up in the police barracks at dawn, with a huge mass of raw meat on the bare table, a dagger stuck into it for me, and of downing enough beer and *tej* to have floated the Sixth Fleet.

We ate our way through the poor ox, and we all danced and sang, and boasted, and drank again, and told each other at great length what brave fellows we all were, and fired off a few rifles to make sure everyone understood this. And to this day, I have no memory whatsoever of getting home, or of how I eventually got there.

I merely remember the next day's hangover.

16

Even the fierce and warlike Danakil tribesmen had caught the festive fever that permeated the town.

Cool and immaculate, quiet and gentle, and showing no signs at all of the last night's frenzies,.Inspector Tafeta was waiting for me when I finally limped over to police headquarters. On the way there I had seen a row of chairs set out in the hot sand just apart from the square, and had recognized some of them as my own; a large hawk had been tearing the stuffing out of my favorite armchair, and a small Ethiopian boy, perhaps six years old, was racing across the sand under the broiling sun with a stick, larger than he was, to drive it away.

I said to Tafeta, grateful for the cool darkness of my whitewashed office: "What's the open-air theater about?"

He smiled. "The Danakil have come in for the Feast Day.

They want to demonstrate their skill with their weapons, and I thought you and your ladies might enjoy it." I liked his use of the word "ladies"; he took it for granted that my wife's friend Dorothy was my concubine, or why else would she be living in our house?

I had visions of archery butts, and of a restful afternoon of lazy semi-interest, like a cricket match, but it was not so. We called the girls together, and a few of the senior officials, and we took our places on the long line of chairs, soiled now with the droppings of hawks, bustards, crows, and anything else that flew over our heads. (The great bustard defacates like a flying cow, and the results are formidable.) There were four or five old-fashioned, overstuffed armchairs, a settee that Tafeta had borrowed from one of the Greek traders, and a dozen or so canvas chairs; all the other spectators—forty or fifty of them, mostly from the police—sat cross-legged on the sand.

We waited.

Tadessa brought over a homemade *hibachi*, a large pot, and all the cups he could find, and made coffee, and we sweated there for an hour or so till at last the warriors appeared, coming from the marketplace in a long column, beating their drums and waving their spears over their heads. As soon as they moved from the shelter of the white adobe houses, and had passed through the ramshackle shelters of the market itself, they moved into their traditional fighting formation, a small group prancing away to each side, the others taking up a V-formation in the center, the chief at their head.

Their aspect was terrifying; they had been working themselves up into a martial frenzy all morning, and it showed. The Danakil are lean and sinuous and wiry, with muscles of the kind usually described as whipcord, and there is a fire in their very black eyes that is alarming. Their hair was frizzled and bushy, the modern Afro hairstyle, and they were dressed, loosely, in supple skins which their women had chewed to the softness of

velvet, or lengths of ochre-colored cloth, with bands of copper
—taken from untended telephone lines—around their upper
arms and their ankles. They carried their little bows and their
short shafts, very limited in range but tipped with arrow poison,
and their staves and spears, and they were moving in a ritual
jog trot to the beat of their drums, the hot red dust rising up
around their bare feet, which were very flat and broad, as they
stomped into it. Their chanting was a soft, incessant ullulation,
growing to a crescendo that was almost hypnotic; it was meant
to warn their enemies of the menace of their appraoch. Two
or three hundred Somalis were following them in a wide arc,
keeping a very respectful distance behind them; for the Somalis
too, this was a *fantasia*, something to get excited about, something that would provide a source of argument for months.

We were all watching them, heads turned, and I was thinking of the frightening potency of their aspect, and of how they
must have inspired terror in the gut of their enemies.

Here, and now, we were their friends; but there was a wild-
ness about them that made you think—as you were supposed
to: *these are savage and very dangerous animals, out for the kill,
and beware . . .*

They pranced from side to side, very lightly, and as they
came closer, it seemed as though their eyes were on fire, a kind
of venom in them you seldom see. The sweat was streaming
off their lean bodies; they moved like leopards, with a graceful
efficiency that no civilized man can ever hope to achieve, the
controlled, taut movements of the perfect animal. All of them
had the split earlobes that signified their first kill, and they wore
the feathers and ivory armbands that commemorated subsequent kills; the slaughter of the largest possible number of their
enemies is the only standard by which a Danakil judges himself
and his fellows; nothing else counts.

They had come, this little group, from their savage desert a
hundred miles and more to the north, driving their camels,

which had been loaded down with salt, packed neatly in cylinders of woven palm fronds, which they would trade patiently in the market here. For food, they had brought along some of their cattle, and they would live exclusively on the milk. And it is interesting to note that here, milking is a two-woman task; the first woman milks the cow, and the second holds the calf close by, for the Ethiopian cow will not give milk unless her calf is there. (If the calf has died, a stuffed skin is used as simulation, and seems to serve the necessary purpose, even when the resulting artifact is nothing more than a crude, straw-stuffed bundle of hide.) The milk is kept in buckets which are also made of woven palm leaves, so tightly knit, so expertly made, that they are less porous than clay *jaras*.

They have no villages, these people. They live six thousand feet below ths great Awash River on one of the hottest plains in the world, where the temperature seldom drops below a hundred and thirty degrees. Their huts are made of long poles, bent into hoops, over which skins are fastened, Somali-fashion, and they will roll up their grass mats, strip down the hoops and coverings, load them on their camels (that ubiquitous desert vehicle), and be on their way in a matter of an hour or less. And the only signs of their passing will be the stone tombs where their slaughtered warriors are buried, round igloos some five feet high with an opening left on one side for the spirit to enter and leave at will.

Their staple food, like that of the Somalis, is milk—but cow's milk; and a standard draught, taken at a gulp, is a gallon or more at a time. They seldom eat meat or grain.

The Danakil have been here for a long, long time—perhaps since the tenth century before Christ. And their ferocious savagery was always so marked that the borders of their territory, even the green highlands, were never settled till the great Galla invasion of the sixteenth century. On these borders— some of them lush and fertile and far better suited to settlement than the surrounding desert—a sort of territorial vacuum had existed, merely because of the fear that the marauding Danakil inspired, even at a distance, among the other tribes. This natural separation kept the Danakil in their original state of Hamitic purity for centuries, a race apart; and it was this vacuum that the equally warlike Gallas seized upon; they simply moved in, and fought.

Even today, the Danakil are a ferocious and quite fearless people. They are physically attractive, with fine features and slender, well-muscled bodies. They somehow give the impression of a steel spring under tension; and they are terrifying.

They came upon us now quite slowly, chanting and dancing and waving their spears. Some of them had drawn the foot-long knife which is their traditional weapon, slightly curved and sharply pointed. (At rest, while their women are, perhaps, milking the cows or churning butter in hide sacks, the men will crouch on their haunches for hours on end, whittling away at a piece of wood or honing their blades to perfection on smooth granite.)

They spread out, facing us, some forty of them, a long and deadly line, their spears loosely held above their heads and weaving gently back and forth.

I said to Tafeta: "I don't see any targets."

He smiled. "No. They won't throw them. These are the stabbing spears, the throwing spears are longer." There was almost a look of mischief in his eyes. He said: "There's something you should know about this. Soon they will dance up to you and jab at your face with their spears, but they won't let them go, there's nothing to worry about. And you mustn't turn your head away. It's very bad if you flinch. The trick, for them, is to get as close to you as they can without actually harming you. For you, the trick is to be absolutely unconcerned. If you can show a little contempt, by grunting perhaps, it would prove to them that you are a very brave man. And that's essential."

I was extremely alarmed about that frenzy; it seemed to border on madness. I tried to assume, without much success, some of Tafeta's nonchalance. I said: "Are they poisoned?" I was just making conversation.

He shook his head and said earnestly: "Oh, no, that's not necessary at all. The blade of a jabbing spear, you see, is long and very narrow. It will go right through a man's skull, or his chest, without any trouble at all. Poison is for arrows only, because with an arrow they can't be so sure of a mortal wound; they're not very accurate."

"And you're quite sure they're not likely to get carried away with their own exuberance? I mean . . ."

He shook his head and said gravely: "No, I don't think so. It would be unforgivable if one of them accidentally killed you. He would lose considerable face."

I tried not to show too much anxiety, if only to impress the ladies; I thought they were enjoying the prospect altogether too much, and I said to Tafeta: "Will they do that to my ladies too?"

He shook his head. "Oh, no, they're women, why should they? To threaten a woman, even in a show like this, would be very unbecoming."

Those damn drums were drowning out our talk; the exercise was about to begin. I said a silent prayer, and sat quite still.

I must admit, the first assault was bearable. One of the men left the line (they were thirty feet away from us) and came charging in to within five or six paces. For a while, he made the ritual threats and gestures, yelling his heart out, the sweat shining on his lithe body while the others shouted encouragements to him. I was thankful, at least, that I could not understand the terrible promises he was making me; the hysterical passion in his eyes was appalling.

And then, scaring me half out of my wits, he dashed up and hurled his javelin at me, a movement so fast I could barely see it. He checked it an inch or two from my forehead, and jabbed it back and forth repeatedly, closer and closer, till it was too close for me to see its point. Each thrust was sharp, incisive, a pointed piston working back and forth, and at each thrust the tone of his yelling rose.

And then he was gone, rushing back to the line while the others cheered him. I looked at Tafeta, and he was nodding wisely, as though to say: "Not bad, not bad at all, but I think the others can do better."

Their women were crouched in the sand, observing us intently, and the young girls were playing with their bangles, slipping them on and off their incredibly narrow wrists; I noticed that the bangles could not have been more than two inches in diameter, yet they slid over those narrow hands with ease.

The next man came up, repeating the performance, and then another and another and another. And by the time four or five of them had been at it, those sharp, shining points, driven forward with incredible speed and force, were reaching so close to the center of my forehead that I could feel the wind of them.

My heart was beating very fast indeed. It's the excitement that matters, and excitement, really, is a loss of control. I reflected, desperately, on the fact that in battle the Danakil are as controlled, in an explosive sort of way, as a man can possibly be; their skill is phenomenal, and skill is a matter of control too. But the sight of those sweating, furious bodies, of the fierce and angry faces, of the murderously ferocious gestures was overwhelming.

Their chief was the most frightening of all, an old, old man so skinny there was hardly a shred of flesh on him, a skeleton of black parchment with sunken cheeks and no teeth at all. When his turn came—the last, thank God, and the best of them all—he scorned to come in as close as the others. He

stood back farther, and shouted louder and with more delibera-
tion, scowling horribly, and then he suddenly yelled "*Khaba!*"
and hurled his whole body at me, shooting his spear arm forward with the speed of a pouncing leopard. The needlepoint
of it (he would have honed it for hours and hours in expectation
of this moment) just lightly touched my skin and then was gone
again. He whirled away at once, and as he turned, it seemed
to me that he was almost laughing. I felt the place he had
touched, and there was the slightest sign of blood on my finger
when I pulled it away.

The old man yelled out an order, and the long line turned
away and began the slow, stately dance back to the village.
Tafeta looked at me and said: "Just a touch of blood. He's very
good, isn't he?"

My wife turned and smiled and took a long, deep breath. She
said, contentedly: "Well, wasn't that exciting?"

*   *   *

The night brought the close of the festivities.

They brought in a dancer for us, a famous woman from
Hargeisa, over the border, to demonstrate an equally famous
dance. In her limited way (the tourist trade has not hit this part
of the world as hard as it has covered North Africa) the Somali
dancer is as specialized in her craft as the better-known Ouled
Naïl of Algeria.

Because of her peculiar callipygian development, the Somali
woman's buttocks stick out with a pronounced upward curve,
and the dancer develops her articulation, from childhood, to
such an extent that the upper surface of her behind becomes,
so to speak, a platform, quite horizontal. (You will see the
beginnings of this among the young girls who, at eight or ten
years old, carry their baby sisters on the hip.) And on this
platform, the dancer will balance a pair of tumblers, one on

229

each cheek. She fills the tumblers (the usual cut-down bottles) with water, places them in position, and then dances. The feet remain still, the arms are held above the head, the bare breasts and the shoulders begin to quiver, and the oscillation gradually builds, moving down the body, till every muscle seems to be rippling; and still not a drop of water is spilled.

Sometimes, by way of variety, the two glasses are placed on the breasts instead. (The breasts of the childless Somali girl are very firm, smooth, and up-pointed.) And now, it is the lower part of the body, and the behind, that moves. The head is thrown back, the chest thrust out, the vessels placed in position, and the shaking begins. Again, it starts lightly, and moves to a rippling crescendo all over the body.

One or the other of these twin forms of the dance can be seen in any major Somali market town; and the skilled performer becomes what is the equivalent to the Western pop idol.

But there was, then, one solitary woman, in the whole of the three Somalilands, who had become very famous indeed because she was able to work with *four* tumblers, two on the behind and two on the breasts, and this was the woman they had produced for us.

She was young, probably about twenty, with a rather flattened face, the nose somewhat broader than is usual among the Somalis. Indeed, her hair style, tightly knit braids clinging close to the skull, the ends elaborately woven, indicated her Galla origins. She wore a splendid necklace of amber beads, filigree silver balls, and brightly colored stones, and a string around her waist from which hung a narrow length of cloth, ochre colored, and nothing else. She had her own personal servant—a girl of ten or twelve years—who carried her dress, a length of brown cotton cloth that she would normally wear wrapped around her waist and thrown up over one shoulder; she was obviously a woman of some consequence. Even the Ethiopians cheered her when she appeared, and the Somalis positively fawned on her, in spite of her sex.

I would not have believed that a woman, any woman, could have taken up the position she adopted to begin the dance: her head thrown back, her chest thrust out and up, her buttocks straining backward, her arms and her legs quite vertical, and the line of her body an incredible S-shape with a straight line above and below. In profile, she looked somewhat like the conventional dollar sign, the straight strokes being her arms and legs, and the S being the precise curve of her torso. A young girl placed the tumblers carefully in position, brimful, and as one of the men began the gentle drumming, she began to quiver.

The quivering, like the sound of the drum, was slight, no more than a vibratiuncle at first. But as the drum came on louder and faster, so did the pulsation of her body become greater and more pronounced, till at last—the drummer beating his soul out—every muscle from her ankles to her neck was throbbing. She held her position, and just *quivered* for fifteen minutes or so.

At last, the diminuendo began. The quivering slowed down, the muscles one by one ceased their trembling until at last she was once more immobile. She raised her head a little, and her eyes were glazed over. The young girl took away the glasses, very gently, and the dancer fell to the ground, exhausted in her own particular coma. She lay on her back, breathing heavily and spasmodically, her arms and legs spread-eagled, her copper-colored body glistening and beginning to tremble again of its own volition, not hers.

She would not move, nor speak, until all of us had gone.

17

The bath in the Dire-Daua house was full of red wine.

I had sent to Djibouti for three demijohns of the excellent *vin ordinaire* they used to sell down there for pennies. It was heavily fortified with Algerian wine, which travels well, but nonetheless was very satisfying as a standard sort of drink for a cool evening on the patio; they had arrived three days ago.

The last time I had done this, each of the huge bottles was down about three inches in the neck; they had been carefully opened and resealed by the policeman who had gone to fetch them for me. He had assumed, I suppose (at least in the early stages of his operation), that I would not notice such a slight discrepancy as he must have made at first. But on the long and boring journey more and more of it had found its way into his stomach, the bottles got lower and lower, and when he arrived he was so drunk that we almost had to pour him off the train; straight into a cell.

This time, I had taken the precaution of sending a Sergeant along instead of a constable. He was a Moslem, at that, and swore he didn't drink. But it was his bright intelligence that had earned him his Sergeant's stripes, and he proved it in his own fashion by unsealing the jars, extracting six or seven bottles of the wine, filling them up again with whatever water was available, and then sealing them up skillfully again. I didn't discover this until a few days later when all the wine, quite naturally, turned sour.

But it was not lost. Lucertola produced, from among his ex-soldier friends, a onetime oenologist of some merit who was now working as a truck driver, and he was delighted to show off his skills as a wine doctor. He emptied the demijohns into the bath, tipped in two buckets full of ordinary slaked lime, stirred it all around, and said cheerfully: "In three days, good again, you see. I come back and strain it for you."

It was, and he did. The Sergeant swore on a stack of Korans that he hadn't touched it, and I thought that the whole matter, ending well, was too trifling a thing to bother with, and so did nothing about it except deliver a stern lecture on the wickedness of stealing, particularly from the Comissioner of Police.

But that was not my week; everything seemed to be going wrong.

First of all, the favorite cheetah, Satan, hanged himself, and nearly died. On the end of his twenty-foot rope, with the heavy log at the other end, he had been prowling around the garden at night waiting for me to come home, and had leaped over the ten-foot stone wall that ran around the property. The log got caught up in some roots, and he hung there, strangling himself, till an alert policeman saw it and came running round to Cloudot's where I was drinking with my Armenian friend, Georj Hadkinjian, who had brought a huge truckload of live crabs up from the coast in British Somaliland, all packed in wet seaweed, and didn't really know how to dispose of them quickly enough. He thought of taking half of them up on the train to Addis Ababa, and wanted a police escort because of some old trouble he'd had with Ras Matara; he didn't get it.

The policeman told me urgently that my cheetah was dangling by the throat from his rope, and we ran around to see what we could do. He was unconscious, still twisting gently, his long legs two feet off the ground. I cut him down, and carried him like a baby into the house, and laid him out on the settee and began to massage his throat and chest.

For a while, I was afraid that he was dead. But soon, he began breathing heavily, and suddenly recovered his wits, lashing out at me with his front paw and then, unexpectedly, using his rear legs like a leopard, driving them hard into my stomach. (I had always believed that Satan was part-leopard; his head was round and solid, on a too-short neck.) But his claws were harmless, and he merely succeeded, once again, in ripping my clothes to shreds and leaving five long gashes down my thigh. And then he was suddenly on his feet and streaking out through the window, like a bolt of lightning. I called him, but he was hiding among the bushes somewhere. And he did not come back into the house until the others, my helpers, had gone.

Then, he curled up at my feet, purring loudly, and licked my hand with a tongue like a rasp. He was all right again.

Poor Satan. He died a little while later, and I thought it must be the result of damage to the throat. But the doctor performed an autopsy on him for me, and told me that it was the measles, which is invariably fatal in felines.

I went back to the office to finish the arbitration which was keeping me there so late in the evening.

An Ethiopian from the Magallo had brought his daughter in to see me, a matter of damages against an Italian mechanic from the trucking company. He was a kind and gentle old man, bowed low with age and poverty, with a kind of helplessness about him, a sort of insecurity that made you, automatically, want to help or at least to sympathize with his seldom-articulated problems. He was alone with his daughter now, he told me, his two sons having been killed in a brush with a Somali hunting party (he swore they killed ten of the Somalis before they died), and his wife having left him for a much younger man.

He was not sure of his daughter's age, but he remembered that she had been born at the time that the Italians, under the cruel and ambitious Marshal Graziano, were reducing Jig-Jigga to ruins with their artillery, and then moving on to do the same to Harar, which had been declared an open city. This was in the early days of May 1936, and the child was therefore eleven years old.

She was small, and very quiet, and rather sweet, a pretty little child dressed in a shapeless once-white shift of crude cotton. It seemed that she had been the mechanic's "servant," and that he had tired of her and had sent her back to the Magallo. The father's case was that since she was no longer a virgin, even at this tender age, the problem of marrying her off was a difficult one; moreover, he thought the Italian ought to pay him something to compensate him for the loss of dignity which was part of the loss of her virginity.

I think it was her *rejection* that troubled him most of all, and the little sadness that it would have caused her, rather than him. I felt a very strong bond between these two quite primitive people; she was stroking his hand gently while he talked, her somber eyes on his, her mouth a little open. There were no tears, there was no anger; there was just the simple insistence that they had been treated badly and should be compensated.

Inspector Gabre was helping me adjudicate this delicate

matter. We searched through our two remaining legal codes together, and found nothing concerning the age of consent. The old man merely wanted ten or twelve Maria Theresas, which I thought would be no problem, but the realization that he would take the money home with him, and then sit silent in his *tukul* with it, and wonder about the future of his pretty little daughter, caused me a great deal of unhappiness.

It was a question of values; the quittance was so slight, and yet he knew that this was all that could be expected in his kind of world.

I asked the girl, through Gabre, what she wanted to do now. She told me promptly that she wanted to look after someone's house for him, a servant again; she could cook, and wash clothes, and sew, and knew how to make European beds. (The servant in Ethiopia, as in most of Africa, is traditionally male, but only at the higher level; lower on the social scale, women are adequate—and they are much cheaper.) The old man agreed that this would be a very happy solution, and could I find her a job?

I sent Gabre over to find the mechanic, and told him to come back either with the man himself or with twenty Maria Theresas, and I wrote a note to Harry Blake and asked him to find some work for the girl in one of the railway administration houses—perhaps his own. I told her to scuttle quickly back to me if it didn't work out, and that I'd do something else about it, though I didn't quite know what.

Gabre came back in no time at all with the twenty dollars, which we handed over to the old man, and the two of them left and walked off down the street hand in hand, a lame old man with a child beside him, walking with great pride and dignity under the yellow street lamps. We stood on the stone steps, Gabre and I, and watched them till they disappeared somewhere down in the riverbed, on their way home to the Magallo.

Gabre laughed and shrugged it all off. But somehow, a touch of melancholy stayed with me long after they had gone.

*   *   *

The next morning, the Diesel engine was stolen out of my ration truck.

It had been on its monthly tour of the territory, carrying food, cigarettes, and the payroll to the men in the tiny outlying stations, and had broken down at a place called Kirireh, about seventy-five miles away, the other side of Harar and the Madar Pass.

This was a very special vehicle. The supply of spare parts was almost nonexistent, and this particular truck had been a broken-down wreck, not running, until Superintendent Michael Evans, in Addis Ababa, had found a brand new motor for it, still in its Turin packing case, tucked away in a forgotten corner of one of the railway warehouses; it had lain there, unnoticed, since the old days of the Italian occupation.

I'd had it sent down on the train, and Sabena had installed it for us, and the newly running truck was one of our most prized possessions. All the other vehicles of our small fleet were held together with baling wire and the cannibal skill of our Italian mechanics, but not this one; this one had an engine that ran smoothly, was completely dependable, and was going to last for years.

Lucertola had brought me the news, and I'd asked him: "How in hell can it break down, it's a brand new motor?"

He had shaken his head. "Not engine trouble. They ran out of spare tires."

(Tires were the greatest problem of all; most of ours were bolt patched and kept alive by the will of God. And on this long monthly journey, the driver carried four, five, six spares, whatever he could lay his hands on.)

I had told Lucertola: "Well, get over there in the breakdown truck, see what you can do."

He had driven off, and now he had returned, this morning, with the news that all was well and that the ration truck was about one hour behind him; he had left it on the road down from Harar, taking it easy on the hairpin bends because the steering left a great deal to be desired.

And an hour and a half later, it turned up.

It was clanking horribly when it drove into the station yard, and I went to see what was wrong, and threw open the hood and stared at the oldest, dirtiest, most broken-down Diesel engine I had ever seen; I was quite shocked. The bearings had gone, the injector was tied on with wire, and there was a very obvious crack in the head.

I sent for Lucerotala and said, fuming: "What the hell happened to our beautiful new motor?"

For a long time he just stared at it, a look of shock on his usually expressionless face. He rubbed some grease off the plate and checked the number uselessly, and said at last: "Well, this isn't it, *Commandante.*"

I said: "I know that, for God's sake. What happened?"

I really believe he was puzzled, as incredulous as I was. He said: "I can't believe it. A couple of hours ago, *due ore fa,* I checked it over, the new motor. Two hours ago!"

"And where was that?"

"On the Harar road, about twenty miles out of town."

"Any other trucks on the road, coming or going? Sabena?"

"No, sir. Nothing either way."

"Or a winch rigged up by the roadside somewhere?"

"Nothing. I just don't believe it. It's impossible."

"But dammit, you don't lift a Diesel engine out of a truck with your bare hands!"

He said stubbornly: "There was nothing on the road. Nothing at all."

238

It was terribly frustrating. The driver, an Italian civilian, swore blind he'd never left the truck. He said he just couldn't account for it and left it at that. His helper, a Somali, also swore they'd been with the truck constantly. And the Ethiopian policeman who was the guard swore black and blue to the same story; they just knew *nothing*.

If only the cooperation between these three mutually suspicious factions had always been so complete! It wasn't often that an Ethiopian policeman would throw in his lot with an Italian; with a Somali, it was even more rare. But somehow or other, they'd conspired to sell off the beautiful new motor, and somehow, they'd gotten away with it. Apart from the railway workshops, there was only one unit in the whole of the territory that was equipped to lug a heavy Diesel engine around, and that was Sabena. And their breakdown crew, they swore, was far away on the road to Ferfer, six hundred miles away across the desert.

It was a mystery; and a very frustrating one.

I locked up all three offenders in the jail, and told them they'd stay there till we found the missing motor. I sent a squad over to Sabena and had them check on engine numbers, and for a week we stopped every ten-ton Diesel we found in the territory.

But by then, I knew, it would be down in Mogadiscio somewhere, being exchanged very profitably for a load of skins, And at the end of three days, when the Governor started getting restless about due process of law, I let the suspects out and put them all back to work. There was nothing else I could do.

We never did find the missing engine, nor figure out just how, in the middle of nowhere, someone had managed to take it out of its chassis, and replace it with another, all in the matter of half an hour.

And then, a sad day in a bad, bad week, Sir Reginald called me over and said unhappily: "I'm afraid they're sending me to Italian Somaliland. I'm the new Governor there."

I could only stare at him.

He said, grimacing: "Mogadiscio, a terribly sophisticated town. A very large staff, a lot of important functions to attend . . . I don't know what to do about Armina. I mean, Mogadiscio, it's . . . it's not like Dire-Daus, half the Colonial Service is there. She can't live with me down there, she can't possibly, She's terribly unhappy about it."

I said: "For God's sake, Reggie, what's happening here? Who's taking over from you?"

He said: "Oh. Yes, of course, that's what I wanted to tell you about. There was a whole batch of cables from London this morning, they're still coming in. It seems we're handing the Territory back to Haile Selassie, just keeping one small part of the Ogaden, the part the French are trying to claim. They're sending some junior out to administer it. It's all . . . it's all a bit of a shock, it's happening so quickly."

I had never seen a man look so miserable.

He said again: "Mogadiscio, what the devil am I going to do in Mogadiscio? Protocol, day and night, no escape from it at all. It's a very considerable promotion, of course, but I don't need promotion, I just want to be left alone. I don't know *what* I'm going to do."

At the moment, I could not sympathize with him. I had worries enough of my own. I said: "What about the police force?"

"Well, Ato Waldo will take over as Governor here, and I suppose he'll bring one of the Emperor's men down from Addis Ababa. We just have to . . . to hand everything over to him."

"And me?"

He said, very worried: "I think they have something for you in Italian Somaliland. District Oficer or something. You have to go to Mogadiscio too, for relocation."

"Oh, my God."

"Yes, it's not a happy prospect, is it? I think they want you in the Somali gendarmerie."

"Oh, Christ!"

The Commandant of the Somali gendarmerie at that time was a man named Lockwood, a rather unprofessional professional soldier. A few months back, when he had been on a pleasure trip to Dire-Daua— unauthorized and uninvited—he had made a drunken nuisance of himself in my town, and I'd had him thrown out; I had simply put him aboard a truck and had him taken back across the border, quite unceremoniously. Now, it seemed, I was to serve under him.

Sir Reginald said again: "What am I going to do about Armina? She's been in tears all morning." He was close to tears himself, and so was I. I don't think I've ever been so unhappy in my life. I had grown to love this town, these people.

I said again: "Oh, Christ."

It seemed as though the bottom had fallen out of everything; there was a horrible, hollow feeling inside me, and I realized how passionately a man can become attached to his surroundings. There were three weeks left for us, and in that time we had to take care of the physical details of the handing-over; it was not a chore that I would look forward to at all, and I wished we could do it right away, there and then, and get the misery of it thrust behind us.

I wondered how the Ethiopians themselves would feel about it. It was, of course, a triumph for them; the United Nations had at last agreed to their demands that their own country be returned to them, and I wondered if their jubilation would show. I wondered if, perhaps—the masters now—they would show any signs of that resentment they must have felt, always, in spite of their courtly acceptance of us.

I left Reggie to his personal worries, and walked slowly round to my headquarters. The news was already all over town, and I simply made it official by posting a sad little notice on the board with the rest of the standing orders.

It was the fast-approaching end of a fascinating tour of duty. And I knew that, at least, part of that fascination lay in the indisputable fact that it had not really been very effective; but then, the most important things in life are always the least consequential.

Nostalgia was already making itself felt, a deep and empty melancholy.

18

The convoy was assembled on the road at the bottom of the hill that led to Harar,

The drivers were all Somalis, heading for the last remaining vestiges, in the Ogaden, of the once Reserved Areas. All the Ethiopians were staying behind.

Most of the British officers were to go to Hargeisa, which they would leave in a few days'—or weeks'—time for England, and the fog and the rain. Some were to be reassigned to Somalia, which was still administered by the British, an ex-enemy territory. A few were on their way to Kenya and civilian life once more.

It was a sorry sight, that pathetic line of vehicles. It may be that I had never before realized just how decrepit our physical presence, of which this sad little convoy was the outward symbol, had been. I had always seen that presence in the cheering light of a lax and gentle nonchalance that now, somehow, looked in retrospect like utter incompetence.

Fords, and Chevies, and Fiat Diesels, with a ten-ton Lancia or two, and an ancient Dodge—there was not one among them that was really road-worthy; those that had come in from the outlying stations even had their tires stuffed with grass, since they were no longer capable of holding air. There was a great deal of baling wire in evidence, and three of the vehicles, non-runners, were being towed. Fortunately there were not many of them, and they were all lightly loaded.

There had been a long and rather disquieting session with Ato Waldo, resplendent in his uniform now. He was still charming and courteous, but there was an underlying severity that I had never seen before. The transfer of authority had been swift and uncomplicated:

"Je demande . . . I demand the whole of the administration stores . . ."

The Governor had said: "Agreed."

"I demand the whole of the railway workshops, with all fittings, furnishings, equipment, and accessories . . ."

"Agreed."

"I demand all the administration vehicles, except those necessary for your transportation over the border . . ."

"Agreed."

"I demand all arms and ammunition except the officers' side arms and the escort rifles . . ."

"Agreed."

"I demand all the administration houses, together with all their furnishings . . ."

"Agreed."

"I demand this . . . I demand that . . . I demand the other . . ."

"Agreed . . . Agreed . . . Agreed . . ."

So it had gone on.

Sir Reginald had been his usual kind and gentle self, and I had been a more or less silent witness. Everything was very stiff and formal, and both sides were even smiling at each other and exchanging little courtesies from time to time. But the careless laxity had gone, as if longtime friends suddenly had to divide an inheritance, and were consequently a little wary of each other.

For two hours, over interminable cups of strong black Harar coffee, the bargaining, completely one-sided, went on; the Governor was under orders, it seemed, to give them everything they wanted. On the police inventory, there was a little awkwardness over fourteen missing pairs of handcuffs; we only had thirty-two pairs all told, and I could not for the life of me remember when any of them had been used. We turned up eighteen of them, and just looked helpless about the rest. And way down on the list, tucked in there somewhere among the trivia, was my little Lancia car. I said, perhaps plaintively: "Can't I keep that? It's not very valuable, you know."

Sir Reginald frowned, and said hesitantly: "Well, I think . . . I think . . ." But Ato Waldo laughed suddenly and said: "Yes, of course, I'm sure that will be all right." We were all friends again.

We all shook hands, and made fatuous comments to each other, and I went for a walk by myself to take one last look at the charming little town.

Cloudot's was still open, but the Armenian café across the street was shuttered; most of the Armenians had hastily closed up everything and had gone to Mogadiscio. There were little groups of Ethiopians, Frenchmen, Italians, and Greeks on the streets—it was very early in the morning—and I found myself crossing the road frequently to avoid contact with people I had known and loved. I felt, strangely perhaps, that it was necessary

245

almost to *sneak* out of the town, out of a territory where we were no longer needed, or perhaps even acceptable.

I went back to the convoy, and Lucertola was there, his pockets bulging with wrenches and screwdrivers. He was scowling at the trucks and saying: "Half of them just aren't going to make it." (And as usual, on matters mechanical, he was right; we left three or four of them scattered over the desert, symbols of finality.)

Sir Reginald headed the convoy out, in the old Dodge, fixed up now but still showing signs of its accident on the Harar road. Armina was with him, in a bright pink dress with the Somali shawl I had once brought her from Jig-Jigga thrown over her shoulders. They had solved their little domestic problem; Armina was going to live in her own house near the Mogadiscio residency, and once the workday was over, and the bemedaled generals had gone home to roost, she would wait there patiently for her lover and console him for his lack of freedom; she seemed quite happy about the arrangement.

My own wife had left already, also for Mogadiscio, to await me there; the last few weeks were rather more than a sensitive soul could tolerate, and we all felt it might be wiser to clear the decks, so to speak, in case of difficulty; but there was none.

I brought up the rear of the convoy in the Lancia, and twenty-five or thirty ancient vehicles set out, with white-robed Ethiops courteously doffing their hats to us as we went by, all very grave and correct. Inspector Gabre, who next to the Governor had been my closest friend there, had given me a large paper bag of *beri-beri*, a potent mixture of powdered peppers, culled from his own farm in the highlands, and it had upset all over the Lancia's upholstery. The day was hot and dusty, the wind blowing in from the deserts to the east where we were headed.

We stopped for lunch in the beautiful Madar Pass, and afterward Reggie said brightly: "I think I'll hurry on ahead now, I'd like to get to Hargeisa before dark. Take care of everything for me, will you? There's a good fellow."

We shook hands, and Armina unexpectedly put her arms around me and kissed me, and off they went to whatever the future was to offer them, back among their beloved Somalis.

It was the last I ever saw of them.

We found water and filled up the steaming radiators, and I sent the convoy on ahead under Michael Evans, and wandered alone around the valley for a little while, the Valley of Despair. I felt it was time, once more, to enjoy the solitude and the silence among the lovely red-sand rocks and the tall pinnacles, to listen for the distant cough of leopard, to seek out the hyrax in their caves, to watch the great flocks of guinea fowl and partridge scratching among the bushes.

But I could not; the enjoyment had quite gone.

The Lancia's fuel pump was giving trouble again, and when I tried to fix it, it broke in two. I tied the reserve five-gallon can of gasoline to the top of the scuttle with a hank of rope, balanced there precariously against the windshield, and fixed a rubber tube down to the carburetor for a gravity feed, and drove off.

*   *   *

There was one more, symptomatic, incident.

At the exit from the pass, where the great plain started and the yellow sand was blowing up in angry little dust devils that twisted this way and that at the whim of the wind, a group of Ethiopians had gathered, four of them in the traditional white *shamma* robes, standing by their mounted leader. I recognized Ras Michael from Lake Hardemeia, my old aquaintance who had driven off our man-eating lions. He was heavily armed now, a Bren gun slung across his back, a .303 Lee-Enfield rifle in his hand, and an ornate dagger stuck in his belt. There were two other men standing a little father away, East Africans, dressed in ragged shorts of military khaki; they were both limping.

The two men were slaves. They would have been caught on this road somewhere, driving their army lorries, years ago perhaps, and would have been enticed into the hills by a scout sent out by Ras Michael. They would have been bribed with a large sum of money to desert with their rifles, and then, on arrival at the chief's village, they would have been hamstrung, the tendon at the back of the knee cut to render them incapable of flight, but still sufficiently mobile to work. Their "advance of pay" would have been taken back, and they would then have been faced with a future of slavery; it was a common enough occurrence in these mountains, a pattern that repeated itself wherever a guerrilla chieftain had access to roads on which, once in a while, the *askaris* of the King's African Rifles passed.

The chief cantered over as I slowed down. His soldiers, also heavily armed, were running lightly, barefoot, at his stirrups. He called out as he dismounted: "Shall we ever see you again?" He was laughing, a bright and friendly man, and his unexpected appearance cheered me up considerably.

I said: "No, I don't suppose so. I'm on my way to Somalia, bloody Somalia."

He grimaced: "That's terrible." There was genuine sympathy in his voice. He said: "Why don't you come with me instead? I could use a British officer or two. And you'd enjoy it, a good life."

I indicated the two East Africans, hovering there. They were hobbling among the Mohr Maddow trees which grew here, slitting the bark like rubber tappers to expose the milk resin, which in two or three months would harden into frankincense and be sent down to Berbera for export.

I said: "Will you promise not to hamstring me?"

He looked at the two ex-*askaris* and watched them for a while. "They're *jambos*, East Africans, they're not people of

248

any consequence." He said, urging me: "Try it for a few months, you can leave whenever you want to. I'll give you command of my army, more than a thousand of them, make you a General."

I wondered if he had stopped the convoy too. But with the Somali rifles on board, and only four soldiers with him, he would have been more prudent. I said: "No, I'd better not."

"It's a fine place, Lake Hardemeia. And you'd be a General, second in command to my Chief of Staff." It all sounded very grand, an army of fire-eating cutthroats ruling their own private mountain. I said: "Not on your life."

He laughed. "No, I didn't really think you would. But you must know it would be better than Somalia."

"I'm damn sure you're right."

"So?"

I shook my head and changed the subject. "May I present you with a hunting rifle?"

He smiled broadly. "You are very kind."

I had two cut-down Lee-Enfields in the car, and I pulled out the better one, its stock lightened and well polished, and gave it to him, holding it out with both hands in the accepted fashion. He took it with both hands too, and bowed gravely. I said: "Perhaps we *will* meet again one day, how can we be sure?"

"Then if you come back, be sure to look for me. Lake Hardemeia, thirty miles north of here."

"I will."

We shook hands, and I drove off again, and when I stopped a mile or so farther down the road to tighten the rope around that damned can of gasoline, he had gone. The soldiers were still there, with the slaves, and they were spread out among the scattered trees, looking, no doubt, for more of the Mohr Maddow.

Beyond the little black specks of their bodies, the reds and the greens of the Madar Pass were vivid in the sunlight. Behind them, in the far, far distance, the mountains were a smoky purple under a cobalt sky, rugged and foreboding, a barrier against the rest of the world. It was empty, and silent, and very beautiful; I thought I had never seen a more beautiful land than this.

In those dark hills, there were Ethiops and Gallas, and Dana-kil and Amhara, and Bejas, Hararis, Guraghes, Agaus, Lastas, Arussis, Boranis, and Shankallas. There were priests and cave-dwellers, peasants and bandits, ancient churches, and tiny round *tukuls*.

It was the home of Prester John and of the violent Theodore, and of Solomon's son Ibna-Malik, son of the King, who later became known as Menelik I, founder of a great and powerful Empire. It was a land of immense fascination.

And once, in the beginnings of history, Sheba slept here.